DISCO

INSIDE ISSUE 1: GENESIS, MARK, 1 & 2 KINGS, JONAH

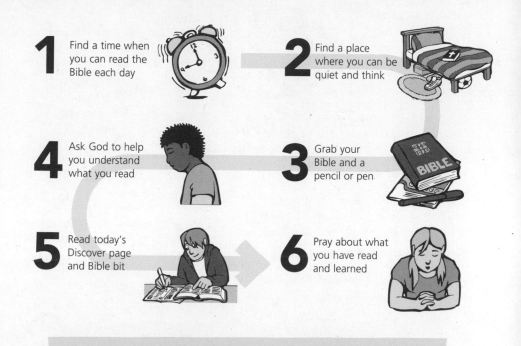

1 Find a time when you can read the Bible each day

2 Find a place where you can be quiet and think

4 Ask God to help you understand what you read

3 Grab your Bible and a pencil or pen

5 Read today's Discover page and Bible bit

6 Pray about what you have read and learned

We want to...

- Explain the Bible clearly to you
- Help you enjoy your Bible
- Encourage you to turn to Jesus
- Help Christians follow Jesus

Discover stands for...

- Total commitment to God's Word, the Bible
- Total commitment to getting its message over to you

Team Discover

Martin Cole, Nicole Carter, Rachel Jones, Kirsty McAllister, Alison Mitchell, André Parker, Ben Woodcraft
Discover is published by The Good Book Company.
thegoodbook.com | thegoodbook.co.uk | thegoodbook.com.au | thegoodbook.co.nz | thegoodbook.co.in
ISBN: 9781784980535 | Printed in India

How to use Discover

Here at Discover, we want you at home to get the most out of reading the Bible. It's how God speaks to us today. And He's got loads of top things to say.

We use the New International Version (NIV) of the Bible. You'll find that the NIV and New King James Version are best for doing the puzzles in Discover.

The Bible has 66 different books in it. So if the notes say…

Read Genesis 1 v 1

…turn to the contents page of your Bible and look down the list of books to see what page Genesis begins on. Turn to that page.

"Genesis 1 v 1" means you need to go to chapter 1 of Genesis, and then find verse 1 of chapter 1 (the verse numbers are the tiny ones). Then jump in and read it!

Here's some other stuff you might come across…

WEIRD WORDS

Sprongle
These boxes explain baffling words or phrases we come across in the Bible.

Think!

This bit usually has a tricky personal question on what you've been reading about.

Action!

Challenges you to put what you've read into action.

Wow!

This section contains a gobsmacking fact that sums up what you've been reading about.

Pray!

Gives you ideas for prayer. Prayer is talking to God. Don't be embarrassed! You can pray in your head if you want to. God still hears you! Even if there isn't a Pray! symbol, it's a good idea to pray about what you've read anyway.

Coming up in Issue 1...

Genesis: Big beginnings

Let's start right at the beginning — the very beginning — in the book of beginnings. The name "Genesis" means "beginnings", and we'll soon see why.

Ever wondered why we're here? Or how life fits together? Or if it matters anyway? Genesis tells us that God was there right at the beginning. In fact, He was there *before* the beginning. And God Himself has always existed, so **He** never even had a beginning!

Confused? You won't be! Just blown away by our amazing God and the incredible plans He has for you.

Mark: All about Jesus

The Gospel of Mark is all about beginnings too. That word "Gospel" means "good news", and Mark tells us in his very first verse that he is writing about "the beginning of the good news about Jesus".

Mark is the shortest of the four life stories of Jesus. (In case you're wondering, the other three Gospels are by Matthew, Luke and John.) Mark races through his story, but packs loads in. He wants us to know just *who* Jesus is and *why* He came. It's gripping stuff!

Elijah: Fiery prophet

We jump into the books of 1 & 2 Kings to meet one of the Bible's most famous prophets: Elijah. A prophet was one of God's special messengers, and Elijah had some epic ways of getting his message across.

Expect battles, soak-the-wood-then-set-it-on-fire competitions and flying chariots! But the message was always the same: God is the one real God, and King of everything — so make sure you listen to Him!

Jonah: The runaway

Imagine being given a special job by God. He has chosen YOU to do it; told you where to go and how to get there; and explained what to say when you arrive. Sounds great? Really exciting? Would you go for it?

Jonah didn't. He took one look at the job in hand, and ran away.

The story of how God dealt with His runaway prophet is exciting, surprising and just a bit scary. Because the heart of the story is how God deals with *everyone* who turns away from Him — and that includes you and me. The heart of it is **grace** — the love and forgiveness God offers to everyone who turns back to Him (even those horrid Ninevites that Jonah didn't want to help in the first place).

Sounds exciting?
Let's dive right in...

Genesis: Big beginnings

**Genesis
1 v 1**

This is the beginning of Issue One of Discover.

So we're going to start with the very beginning of the Bible — Genesis.

It's the beginning of the awesome story of the universe that God created.

We'll find out how He did it and how we fit into it!

GENESIS FACTS

1 Genesis means "beginnings"

2 It tells us about the beginning of the universe

3 …and the beginning of human beings

4 …and the beginning of sin in the world

5 …and the beginning of God's special people — the Israelites.

Read Genesis 1 v 1

Before anything else existed, someone was already there. It's hard to understand that God had no beginning. Unlike us puny humans, He has always existed!

What did God do? Go back one letter (B=A, C=B, D=C) to find out.

— — —

H P E

— — — — — —

D S F B U F E

— — —

U I F

— — — — — — —

I F B W F O T

— — —   — — —

B O E   **U I F**

— — — — —

F B S U I

That means God created EVERYTHING! He created the whole universe from nothing. And He is in total control of it.

What does this tell us about God? Add your own thoughts to the bottom two answers.

God is great

God is powerful

God is _____

God is _____

_____

Pray!

On scrap paper, write down a list of some of the things God has created. Now spend time praising Him for everything He has made.

Light switch

**Genesis
1 v 2-13**

Close your eyes and cover your ears, then silently count to ten.

Imagine a world like that — empty, dark and silent.

WEIRD WORDS

Formless
Had no shape

Spirit of God
The Holy Spirit. He was around at the beginning, and He's around now, helping Christians to live for God.

Vault
Gap or space

Now read Genesis 1 v 2

What was the earth like at the very beginning?

- colourful ☐
- empty ☐
- like it is now ☐
- totally dark ☐
- formless ☐
- full of stuff ☐

The world was totally dark and empty. Then God spoke…

DAY 1

Read verses 3-5

and fill in the vowels (aeiou) to reveal what God said.

L__t th__r__
b__ l__ght (v3)

It was the very first day in the history of the world! God spoke. Just a few words from Him was enough to make light burst into an empty world.

DAY 2

Read verses 6-8

L__t th__r__ b__ a
vault to s__p__r__t__
th__ w__t__rs (v6).

God created the sky. Just like that!

DAY 3
Read verses 9-13

On the 3rd day, God created
l__nd and s__ __ (v10),
pl__nts and tr__ __s giving
us fr__ __t and
v__g__t__bl__s (v11). God
made all of this and was
pleased with it (v12).

Pray!

Praise and thank God for the world He has made.

3

Stars, starfish & starlings

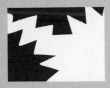

We're way back at the beginning of the universe.

So far God has made the world, giving it light, land, sea and plants.

It's time for Him to make some bigger stuff...

WEIRD WORDS

Sacred times
Special times/seasons set aside for God

Blessed
Given a special job by God

Be fruitful
Have lots of babies!

DAY 4

Read Genesis 1 v 14-19

Think how tiny you are compared with the moon and the sun and all the millions of stars out there in space.

God made the sun, moon and stars. Think how **awesome and powerful** He must be! And yet we can personally know this incredible God!

Unjumble the anagrams to reveal what the sun, moon and stars control (v14).

S_____ times,
A D S R E C

D_____ and
S A D Y

Y_____
R A S E Y

Astronomers have discovered that there is a pattern to where the sun, moon and stars are in relation to the earth. And that's how we work out the length of days, months and years. God made them and controls their movements!

DAY 5

Read verses 20-23

*On spare paper, write a list of all the fish and animals you can think of that live in the **sea**. Now write down another list of all the different **birds** you can think of.*

God created all of those creatures and thousands more! They didn't come into existence by accident. God planned it, and what He made is great!

If you have time, check out **Psalm 8**. It's a song King David wrote, praising God for all the amazing things He created.

Pray!

When you pray, you're talking to God who created everything! Think of some of your favourite things in the universe. Stars? Snakes? Snow? Strawberries? Sea horses? Thank God for making them. You could use Psalm 8 as a prayer to God.

God's masterpiece

**Genesis
1 v 24-31**

It's day 6 of creation, and it's time for God to create animals: cats, bats, rats, gnats, frogs, dogs, elephants, anteaters, duck-billed platypi, lions, tigers, monkeys, and yes, even slugs.

WEIRD WORDS

Livestock
Animals used either for work or food (like sheep, camels, horses)

Be fruitful
Have loads of children!

Subdue
Rule over

DAY 6

Read Genesis 1 v 24-25

God made every kind of animal. And now everything was ready for the most important part of creation… God's masterpiece — us!

Read verses 26-27

and cross out all the Xs to discover an amazing fact.

XGOXXDCREXXAXTE
XDMENANXDWOXXMEXX
NINXXHIXSIXMAXGEXX

G_____

_____

_____

Wow!

We're created to be a picture of what God is like! How awesome is that?! YOU show something of what God is like! And that's not all…

Read verses 28-31

What task did God give to humans? (v28)

XXRUXLEXXOXVEXRA
XLLLXIVXINXXGCREXX
AXTUXREXSXX

R_____

_____

Think!

God has put us in charge of His world! To look after it and enjoy it. We are God's chosen rulers of this world.

What can you do to look after God's world? Drop less litter, recycle, plant trees?

Pray!

Thank God that you're so special to Him; that He made you to be like Him; and that He's given you a world to look after.

Time to relax

5

*God has finished
creating the
whole universe.*

*So what will He
do next?*

In the wordsearch, find 14 things
God created (they can all be found
in Genesis chapter 1).

```
A Y U T R E E S C J
Z N X W S L S K H L
L I I N V B T Y Z A
Y G Q M E K F G P N
W H U M A N S U L D
M T X J M L R F A P
O C T M F E S U N O
O S D R I B E I T G
N D P B S T A R S N
V R H Q H O A D A Y
```

Read Genesis 2 v 1-3

God didn't rest because He was
tired! But because He had made
everything that could possibly need
making, and He saw that it was all
very good!

God rested on the seventh day, and
He made it a special holy day (v3).
Many Christians have Sunday as
their holy day, when they rest from
work.

Go forward 3 letters to reveal what
God did on the seventh day.

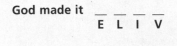

God _ _ _ _ _ _
    O B P Q B A

That's why, on Sundays, many
Christians take a break from all the
work they do.

God made it _ _ _ _ _
    E L I V

That's why many Christians keep
Sunday for God. Do you take extra
time out to talk to God and read
the Bible?

Wow!

But God doesn't promise us
a rest just one day a week.

For everyone who trusts in
Jesus, He's promised a much longer
rest — with Him, for ever, in eternal
life!

Action!

Do you make sure you rest one
day a week? It's good to set aside
a day where you don't do school
work or other busy things. You
can use it to enjoy God's creation
and give Him more of your time.
How can you change your Sunday
so that it's holy — set apart for
God?

WEIRD WORDS

Vast array
Their hugeness and
all their different
parts

Blessed
Made special

Holy
Set apart for God

Answers: animals, moon, night, birds, trees, humans, fish, sea, sky, day, sun, stars, plants, land

Dust for starters

**Genesis
2 v 4-7**

*Human beings
are incredibly
complicated
things.*

*We can see,
feel, breathe,
talk, walk — do
loads of amazing
things and it's no
problem to us.*

Yet we're made up of thousands of complicated parts.

Let's see how well you know your body. Draw lines to match up the body parts with what they do.

1. Heart

2. Lungs

3. Larynx (voicebox)

4. Liver

5. Stomach

6. Tibia & fibula

A. Helps you to talk

B. Help you to breathe

C. Help you to walk

D. Pumps blood around your body

E. Cleans your blood

F. Stores food & breaks it down

So how did God make something as complicated as a human?

Read Genesis 2 v 4-7

**God made man from the
d_____ of the ground!**

You've probably learned in science lessons a bit about the amazing way our bodies work. But **God** could create all this complicated stuff out of **dust**!

God designed each tiny part of our bodies and, with no trouble at all, created the whole human race! It's mind-blowing!

Read verse 7 again

Wow!

Just as Adam needed God to breathe life into him, we depend on God for our every breath. Without Him we couldn't exist!

Pray!

Thank God for giving you life. Praise Him for three top things your body allows you to do.

WEIRD WORDS

Account
Report

The heavens and the earth
All things. God made everything!

Shrub
Small plant

Answers: 1-D, 2-B, 3-A, 4-E, 5-F, 6-C

1

Genesis 2 v 8-17

Do you like sitting in the garden in summer?

Or do you find gardens really boring?

Today we look at a garden that anyone would love to hang out in.

WEIRD WORDS

Headwaters
Upper parts of the rivers

Aromatic resin
Perfume

Onyx
Precious stone

Garden of freedom

Read Genesis 2 v 8-14

God made a beautiful garden filled with wonderful plants, refreshing rivers and trees producing tasty fruit. Paradise! And he let Adam live in it. Perfect.

Use the code to show which two trees are given a specific mention.

The tree of _ _ _ _ _ (v9)

God gave Adam the tree of life showing that his friendship with God could last for ever.

The tree of the

_ _ _ _ _ _ _ _ _

_ _ _ _ _ _ _ (v9)

If Adam ate the fruit of this tree, he would decide for himself what's right and wrong. But that's God's job!

Read verse 15

God put Adam in the garden to work in it and take care of it. He gave Adam an important job — protecting God's wonderful creation.

Read verses 16-17

God made a rule to protect Adam: "Don't eat from the tree of the knowledge of good and evil". God gave Adam a choice:

Obey God and live with Him for ever

OR

Disobey God, eat from the tree, and die

Think & pray!

We can turn our backs on God and live our own way. Or, through Jesus, we can live to please God. Ask Him to help you make the right choice.

A C D E F G I K L N O R T V W

8

Spare rib

**Genesis
2 v 18-25**

*The first man,
Adam, was living
in God's perfect
garden.*

*But something
was missing…*

Read Genesis 2 v 18

and fill in what God said.

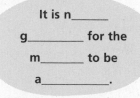

It is n_____

g_____ for the

m_____ to be

a_____.

Read verses 19-20

Can you imagine that? Having to
name all of those creatures, looking
to see if any of them could be your
"mate"! Fancy marrying a skunk?
Or a hippo?!

Unsurprisingly, Adam's search for
a partner was unsuccessful. God
had made the animals completely
different from the man, so none of
them could be Adam's companion.
Only the man was made in **God's
image**.

**Now read verses 21-25
for God's great solution.**

God made a

w_____ from

Adam's r_____ (v22)

The woman (Eve) was just what
Adam wanted! Someone like him,
an equal, so she understood him.
Yet she wasn't exactly the same as
Adam, and added to his life. The
perfect companion.

Adam's wife was very special to
him, because she came from his
own body.

Wow!

God says all marriages
are very special. Two people come
together and form one partnership
(v24).

Pray!

Thank God for creating both
men and women. Thank Him for
His gift of marriage. And pray
for people you know who are
married. That God will help them
to serve Him together.

WEIRD WORDS

Livestock
Animals used either
for work or food
(like sheep, camels,
horses)

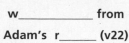

9

Genesis 3 v 1-7

God made Eve, the perfect partner for Adam.

They lived together in God's garden, looking after His creation.

They only had one rule to obey — don't eat from the tree of the knowledge of good and evil.

WEIRD WORDS

Crafty
Sneaky

Snake charmer

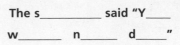

*Today's missing words are written **backwards**, so you'll have to unjumble them first.*

ton	tiurf	tae
yllaer	evag	ekans
madA	eert	lliw
uoY	eid	nedrag

Read Genesis 3 v 1

The snake said "Did God
r_____ say you can't
e_____ from any t_____
in the g_____?"

The snake was the devil in disguise! He tricked Eve into doubting what God had said.

Wow!

The devil tricks us into doubting what God says in the Bible. "Has God really forgiven me?" "Is that sin really wrong?" He uses all sorts of tricks to get us doubting God. It might be what friends or family say to us, or stuff we watch or read. If you're unsure about something, check out what the Bible says about it. God doesn't lie!

"Am I really a Christian?" "How can God love me when I keep sinning?" If you have doubts like these, ask for the free leaflet on DEALING WITH DOUBTS. Email us at discover@ thegoodbook.co.uk

Read verses 2-5

The s_____ said "Y____
w_____ n_____ d____."

The devil lied to Eve, suggesting that God was tricking her! And that if she ate the fruit she could be as powerful as God! All lies.

Read verses 6-7

Eve ate the f_____, then
g_____ some to A_____.

Adam and Eve **disobeyed** God, breaking His only rule. Eating fruit from that tree meant they were deciding for themselves what was right or wrong. But that's God's job. They wanted to **be God**. They wanted to live their own way, instead of God's way. That's called **sin**.

Pray!

Ask God to help you not to listen to the devil's lies. And to obey God, living His way instead of living your own way.

From bad to curse

**Genesis
3 v 8-19**

*Get your brain
in gear, because
God's got loads to
teach us today.*

*Fill in the blanks
with vowels
(aeiou), then read
the facts.*

WEIRD WORDS

Enmity
Hatred

Offspring
Children

Childbearing
Having babies

Toil
Hard work

Read Genesis 3 v 8-13

1. Ad__m   __nd Ev__
   h__d fr__m G__d

They knew they'd disobeyed God,
so they tried to hide from Him. Then
they tried blaming each other and
the snake for their sin.

When we do wrong, we often think
we can get away with it. Or we try
blaming other people. But we can't
hide anything from God. And we
can't blame anyone else for our sin.

Right from the beginning, God
punished those who sinned against
Him…

Read verses 14-15

2. G__d c__rs__d
   th__ sn__k__

The snake would be hated by
people and made to crawl.

Read verse 16

3. G__d p__n__sh__d
   __v__

Because Eve disobeyed God, women
suffer pain in giving birth. And Eve
would have tough times with her
husband.

Read verses 17-19

4. G__d p__n__sh__d
   __d__m

Men would have to work hard to
grow enough food to eat.

But it's not all bad news…

Read verse 15 again

5. Eve's __ffspr__ng w__ll
   cr__sh th__ sn__k__'s
   h__ __d!

It sounds weird, but God promised
that one of Eve's family would one
day beat the devil (the snake)! This
promise is all about JESUS, who
would come to earth to beat sin and
the devil for ever!

Pray!

Ask God to help you not to
listen to the devil's lies. And
to obey God, living His way
instead of living your own way.

Thrown out of Eden

**Genesis
3 v 20-24**

*Adam and Eve
disobeyed God,
and they deserved
to be punished.*

*But God had
good news for
them as well as
bad news!*

WEIRD WORDS

**Garments
of skin**
Clothes made of
animal skins

Banished
Threw him out

Cherubim
Angel-like creatures

Read Genesis 3 v 20

then go back one letter.

Good news!

F W F   X B T

U I F   N P U I F S

P G   B M M   U I F

M J W J O H

All humans are descended from
Eve. What an amazing privilege for
her!

Read verse 21

Good news!

H P E   H B W F

U I F N

D M P U I F T

They'd sinned against God, yet He
still looked after them!

Read verses 22-24

Bad news!

1. _ _ _ _ _
   E F B U I

2. _ _ _ _ _ _ _ _
   T F Q B S B U F E

   _ _ _ _   _ _ _
   G S P N   H P E

Adam and Eve were not allowed
to eat from the tree of life, so
they couldn't live for ever. Even
worse, they were thrown out of the
garden, so they could no longer live
with God.

Sin separates us from God. And,
because we all disobey God
sometimes, we're all separated from
Him. We all deserve punishment for
our sin.

Good news!

Read point 5 from yesterday's
Discover. JESUS can rescue us
from the punishment we deserve.
He died to take the punishment in
our place.
If we trust in Him, we can go to
live with God for ever!

Want to know how our sins can be
forgiven by Jesus? Write in for the
free booklet *What's it all about?*
Email: discover@thegoodbook.co.uk

Elijah: Fiery prophet

**1 Kings
16 v 29-34**

We're now going to take a look at the book of 1 Kings.

Remember King David (who killed Goliath)? He was a king who served God.

The books of 1 & 2 Kings tell us about the Israelite kings who ruled after King David died.

HISTORY STUFF

- David's son, **Solomon**, started off as a godly king but he turned away from God.

- The Israelites were then split into two kingdoms. The northern one was known as **Israel** and the southern one was **Judah**.

- The books 1 & 2 Kings tell us the history of the two Israelite kingdoms — which kings served God and which ones turned the people away from the Lord.

We're mainly going to look at the northern nation, **Israel**. As we join the story, Israel has had four kings since David. If you have time, you can read about all these kings in 1 Kings chapters 1-16.

And if you think those kings were bad, check out this one…

Read 1 Kings 16 v 29-34

and fill in the vowels (aeiou) to show just how evil Ahab was.

He did more __v__l
than any of the k__ngs
b__f__r__ h__m (v30)

He w__rsh__pp__d
false gods like B__ __l and
__sh__r__h (v32-33)

He did more to
arouse the __ng__r of the
L__rd than any other
k__ng of __sr__ __l (v33)

Think!

God hates it when we make other things more important than Him (see Exodus 20 v 3-6). Is there anything **you** worship more than God?

Ahab was the most evil king of Israel. **But God cared for the Israelites**. So He would send someone to warn them to turn back to Him.

More about this mysterious messenger tomorrow…

**1 Kings
17 v 1-6**

Ahab

Yesterday we met Ahab, the most evil king Israel had ever had.

Will God put up with his sinful ways?

Raven mad

No chance! He sent Elijah the prophet to tell Ahab what's what.

God's people & God's prophet

The Israelites were **God's people**. He promised to be faithful to them and look after them. Their part of the covenant agreement was to obey God's laws.

But the Israelites kept **rejecting God** and disobeying His laws. So God sent His messenger, Elijah, to tell the Israelites (and their king) to turn back to God and start living for Him.

Read 1 Kings 17 v 1

What was Elijah's message from God? Go back 1 letter to find out.

U I F S F

X J M M C F O P

E F X P S

S B J O J O

U I F O F Y U

G F X Z F B S T

V O U J M J

T B Z T P

Why no rain?

1. God's promise

Look up **Deuteronomy 11 v 16-17**. God said that if the people worshipped other gods, then He would stop the rain.

2. Rain was vital

In such a hot, dry country, rain was vital to help their crops grow so they had enough food.

3. God bashed Baal

Ahab worshipped Baal, who was supposedly the god of rain and storms. By stopping the rain, God showed that Baal was fake and powerless.

Read verses 2-6

Elijah was in danger from King Ahab. So God told him to hide out for a while. Elijah obeyed God's instructions, and the Lord sent ravens to bring him food!

Pray!

God cares for His people. He wanted the Israelites to turn back to Him, and He looked after Elijah in an amazing way. Thank God that He cares so much for His people.

Widow of opportunity

**1 Kings
17 v 7-24**

Elijah told King Ahab there'd be no rain until God said so.

Now Elijah is hiding from Ahab and God is sending ravens to bring him food!

And he's drinking water from a little stream.

WEIRD WORDS

Gathering sticks
To make a fire to bake the bread

Read 1 Kings 17 v 7-9

God told Elijah to go to Zarephath. Zarephath was outside of Israel and was a place where Baal was worshipped. But the Israelites were rejecting God, so He sent Elijah to a non-Israelite widow.

Wow!

God cares for everyone and wants everyone to be part of His people. Even the person you think would never become a Christian.

Read verses 10-16

The woman and her son were very poor and were down to their last meal. Yet Elijah asked her to bake him some bread! But what was his great promise to her?

The jar of f_____ will not r_____ out, and the j_____ of _____I will not run dry until the Lord gives r_____ on the land (v14)

She trusted Elijah, and the Lord gave the woman and her son enough food to stay alive!

Read verses 17-18

She blamed Elijah and God for her son's illness. Ever blame God for bad stuff that happens? Yet His plans are perfect, and we fail to see how He uses such terrible times to do amazing things.

Read verses 19-24

God brought the lad back to life! His mum's opinion of God completely changed.

What did she say to Elijah?

Now I know that you are a m_____ of G_____ and that the word of the L_____ from your mouth is the t_____ (v24).

Wow!

God is in control of everything and is totally trustable. He longs for us to trust His word and to rely on Him.

Pray!

Thank God that we can read His word in the Bible, and that it's both true and powerful!

Prophet protector

**1 Kings
18 v 1-15**

King Ahab and the Israelites worshipped Baal instead of God.

So God punished them by sending no rain for three whole years!

WEIRD WORDS

Devout
Devoted to God

Jezebel
Evil wife of Ahab

Prophets
Messengers

Mules
Half horse, half donkey

Spirit of the Lord
The Holy Spirit

Read 1 Kings 18 v 1

Elijah had been hiding from Ahab for three years, and Ahab had searched everywhere for him, wanting to kill him. Ahab was an enemy of God. And his wife Jezebel killed many of God's prophets. But now God sent Elijah to meet evil Ahab.

Yet not all of Ahab's men were enemies of God…

Read verses 2-4

What had Obadiah done?

a) killed 100 prophets ☐

b) rescued 100 prophets ☐

c) rescued 100 porcupines ☐

What a brave thing to do! Obadiah was working for King Ahab, yet he secretly went against the king and hid 100 of God's prophets in caves!

Read verses 5-6

What was Obadiah looking for?

a) grapes for the animals ☐

b) grass for the animals ☐

c) Elijah the prophet ☐

He was looking for b but found c!

Read verses 7-15

Why didn't Obadiah want to do what Elijah asked him?

a) Ahab would kill him ☐

b) A hat would kill him ☐

c) Ahab would kiss him ☐

Obadiah was worried that Elijah would run off and hide again. Then Ahab would be furious with Obadiah and kill him. But Elijah promised not to. Tomorrow we'll see what happened…

ELIJAH	OBADIAH
was God's messenger and boldly told people what God had to say.	served God secretly. He wasn't loud about it but he bravely saved 100 prophets.

Wow!

Elijah and Obadiah served God in different ways. Some Christians serve God loudly, leading meetings. Others serve God quietly, getting on with things behind the scenes.

Pray!

Ask God to show you how you can serve Him best.

Baal game

**1 Kings
18 v 16-29**

*God's prophet
Elijah is finally
going to meet
evil King Ahab
again.*

*And there's
going to be a
big showdown
between God
and Baal...*

WEIRD WORDS

Baals/Asherah
Fake gods

Jezebel
Ahab's evil wife

Read 1 Kings 18 v 16-19
What did Ahab call Elijah? (v17)

But it was Ahab who'd caused
trouble for Israel by turning away
from God and worshipping Baal.
God had punished them by not
sending rain for three years.

Read verses 20-21
*Follow the spiral to reveal Elijah's
challenge to the people.*

HOW LONG WILL YOU WAVER BETWEEN 2 OPINIONS? IF THE LORD IS GOD FOLLOW HIM BUT IF BAAL IS GOD FOLLOW HIM

H _____
_____
_____
_____
_____
_____
_____
_____

Think!
Do you sit on the fence like these
people? Can't decide whether or
not to trust in Jesus? You can't keep
putting off the decision for ever!

Action!
Or maybe you've got friends who
go to church but aren't Christians?
Is there anything you can (helpfully!)
do or say to get them thinking?

Read verses 22-29
Elijah set a test for Baal and God.
Whoever could set the meat
on fire is the true God. Baal's
prophets screamed, shouted and
cut themselves, but Baal wouldn't
answer.

Wow!

There's only one true God. So
it's a waste of time worshipping
anything else. Is it time for you to
get off that fence and start living
for God?

Tomorrow: It's God's turn...

Pours for thought

1 Kings 18 v 30-37

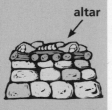

altar

Elijah set a test for Baal and for God.

Whoever could set the sacrifices on fire was the true God.

Yesterday we saw how Baal failed miserably. Of course he did; he's a fake god who doesn't exist!

Read 1 Kings 18 v 30-32

Elijah rebuilt God's altar using twelve stones. *What did the twelve stones stand for?*

Go back one letter to find out.

— — — — — —
U X F M W F

— — — — — — — —
U S J C F T P G

— — — — — —
J T S B F M

Elijah was reminding the Israelites that the Lord was their God. The Lord had made a covenant agreement that He'd protect them, bless them and give them land. But they'd broken the agreement by disobeying Him. Yet He was willing to forgive them if they'd just turn back to Him.

Read verses 33-37

Why pour water on the wood, making it harder to set fire?

— — — — — — — — — —
O P U I J O H J T

— — — — — — — —
U P P I B S E

— — — — — — !
G P S H P E

Elijah wanted to show just how powerful God is. To prove that He's the **only true God**. *What else did Elijah ask God to do?*

— — — — — — —
U V S O U I F

— — — — — — — — — —
J T S B F M J U F T

— — — — — — — — —
C B D L U P I J N

Think!

Do you know anyone who needs to turn back to God? Maybe even you?

Pray!

Ask God to change their lives around, so they start living for Him again. Remember, nothing is too hard for God!

Tomorrow: The big finale!

18

Fire proof

**1 Kings
18 v 38-46**

*Fake god Baal
couldn't set fire
to the sacrifice.*

*Could God do
it — even though
Elisha had poured
water all over the
wood?*

WEIRD WORDS

Sacrifice
Gift of meat offered
to God to make
peace with Him

Fell prostrate
Fell flat on their
faces, out of respect
for God!

Carmel
The mountain where
God had sent fire

Read 1 Kings 18 v 38-39

Of course the Lord could do it —
He's the only true God! Finally, the
Israelites realised this too.

*To reveal what they said, cross out
all the As, Bs & Cs and follow the
maze.*

A	A	E	L	O	R	B	C
T	H	B	A	D	C	A	
C	B	C	C	A	H	E	B
A	A	B	C	B	A	I	C
B	C	!	D	O	G	S	A

T _____
_____ ! (v39)

The Israelites turned back to God
and He forgave them!

But read verse 40

These Baal-worshippers had not
turned to God. In fact they'd led
the people away from God, so they
were rightly punished for their sin.

Wow!

God will forgive anyone who turns
to Him and turns away from sin. But
anyone who refuses to live for God
and trust in Jesus will one day be
punished for ever in hell.

Read verses 41-46

More good news for the Israelites!
Remember how God had stopped
the rain for three years because
Ahab and the people worshipped
Baal? Well, Elijah now prayed to
God (v42) and the Lord sent rain! So
the crops would grow again and the
people could eat!

Wow!

God is trustworthy — He keeps His
promises. And He's so generous,
He gives us more than we deserve.
He even gave King Ahab another
reminder to turn to Him, by showing
His power through Elijah's speedy
legs! (v46)

Pray!

How many of these can you
praise God for right now?
• Being the only God
• Being generous and trustworthy
• Helping you turn to Him
• Forgiving you

Prayer pointers

James
5 v 13-18

As we've seen, God used Elijah to do great things.

900 years later, James wrote about him...

WEIRD WORDS

Elders
Church leaders

Anoint them with oil
Pour oil on their head as a sign of God's healing

Righteous person
Someone who is right with God, and puts God first

Earnestly
Seriously

Think!

What do you do to cope when life seems tough?

_____

_____

And what about when you're happy? How do you show it?

_____

_____

Read James 5 v 13-16

Draw lines to match up the situations with how James says we should react to them.

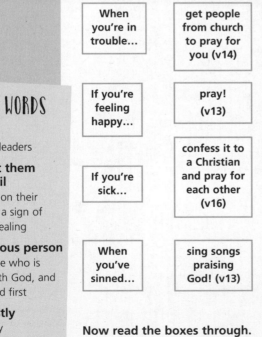

When you're in trouble...	get people from church to pray for you (v14)
If you're feeling happy...	pray! (v13)
If you're sick...	confess it to a Christian and pray for each other (v16)
When you've sinned...	sing songs praising God! (v13)

Now read the boxes through.

Wow!

Get the picture? Whatever situation you're in, talk to God about it! Praise Him when you're happy, turn to Him when life stinks, and say sorry when you've done wrong. God longs to hear you talk to Him!

Read verses 17-18

Elijah is a great example of someone who prayed loads. He prayed for the rain to stop and God stopped it, punishing the Israelites for rejecting Him. When they turned back to God, Elijah prayed for God to send rain again. And He did!

Pray!

On scrap paper, write down things you can praise God for, stuff you need Him to sort out in your life, and people who need God's help right now. Talk to God about these things.

On the run

**1 Kings
19 v 1-8**

*With God's help,
Elijah stood up
to evil King Ahab
and the 450
prophets of Baal.*

*Surely nothing
can stop him
now!*

Er, think again...

WEIRD WORDS

Jezebel
Ahab's wife

Judah
See the history stuff
on day 12

Broom bush
Desert plant

Horeb
The mountain where
God gave Moses the
10 Commandments

Read 1 Kings 19 v 1-4

Elijah has just proved that the Lord
is the only God, and that Baal is
useless. Yet he was scared stiff by
Jezebel's threats and ran away into
the desert.

*Fill in the missing letters to show
what Elijah forgot to do.*

Jezebel		old Elijah
You'll die tomor		ow.
She wanted to m		rder him!
Elijah was		cared.
He did no		turn to God
& made up his m		nd
to ru		away.
He ran a lon		way,
to a t		wn
in Ju		ah

Elijah did not

But it wasn't just fear that made
Elijah give up and want to die.
He was also exhausted after all that
he'd been through.

Wow!

It's often when
something great has happened to
us that the devil tries to tempt us to
mess up.

Or when we're exhausted, he
tempts us to give up. We need to
ask God to give us strength at such
times.

Read verses 5-8

God wouldn't let Elijah give up! He
gave Elijah bread and water so he
had enough strength to keep going.
Enough strength to travel for 40
days! (v8)

Wow!

God is so good to His people. He
gives them so much more than they
expect or deserve!

Pray!

Ask God to give you strength to
serve Him, and not to give up
when the devil tempts you.

For a fact sheet on "Facing tough
times" email
discover@thegoodbook.co.uk
or check out
www.thegoodbook.co.uk/contact-us
to find our UK mailing address.

Wind or whisper?

21

**1 Kings
19 v 9-18**

*Elijah ran away
to the desert,
to hide from
Jezebel, who
wanted to kill
him.*

*God kept him
alive, and now
Elijah is hiding
out in a cave...*

WEIRD WORDS

Zealous
Enthusiastic

Hazael
Would become
King of Aram and
attack Israel

Jehu
Would destroy
Ahab's family

Elisha
Would take over
from Elijah

Read 1 Kings 19 v 9-10

Elijah told God how the Israelites
were disobeying Him in a big way.
Elijah felt as if he was the only godly
person left. He felt as if he was
serving God all alone.

Read verses 11-13

and unjumble the anagrams.

A terrifyingly powerful

w_____ tore apart the
   d i w n

m_____ and
   a n o u n m i s t

shattered the r_____.
        c o r k s

But God was n_____ **in the**
        t o n

wind. Then came an

e_____
   t h e e a r q u a k

and a f_____, **but the**
      r i f e

Lord was not in those.

Finally there was a gentle

w_____ **and God**
   w e r s h i p

spoke to Elijah.

Wow!

We often expect God
to speak to us through
spectacular things, and sometimes
He does! But He mostly speaks
quietly, through His Word.

For Elijah, that meant a voice. For
us, it means the Bible.

Action!

As you read the Bible this week,
look out for how God is speaking
to you. You could even write down
what you've learned in a notebook.

Read verses 14-18

Elijah still wanted to punish the
Israelites. So God told him to
appoint three men who would
punish King Ahab and the Israelites.

Yet even though the Israelites had
repeatedly rejected Him, God would
still keep 7000 people safe (v18)!

Pray!

Thank God that He speaks to us
through His Word, the Bible. And
thank Him that He's so forgiving,
even though we've let Him down
so many times.

Farewell to farming

**1 Kings
19 v 19-21**

*Read 1 Kings 19
v 19-21.*

*Now use the
word pool to
fill in the news
report.*

WEIRD WORDS

**Twelve yoke of
oxen**
24 strong bulls, used
to pull ploughs

---

cloak   family   burned
messenger   Elijah   Shaphat
prophet   people   ploughing
oxen   Elisha   servant

RICH FARMER THROWS IT ALL AWAY

In surprising news, E_____,
son of wealthy farmer
S_____, has turned
his back on the f_____
business. Instead, he has taken
the post of s_____
to E_____, the famous
p_____.

When asked why he took such a
low-paying job, Elisha said "Elijah
came up and threw his c_____
around me to show that one
day I'll take his place as God's
m_____".

To show he was serious about his
career change, Elisha b_____
all his p_____ equipment
and turned his o_____ into steaks
for the p_____!

Wow!

Like Elisha, God calls us to leave our
old lives behind and follow Him. To
turn away from our sinful ways. To
turn our backs on the stuff that's
more important to us than God.

Think!

Maybe there's a sin that
you keep falling into. Or something
that's more important to you than
God is. What things do you need to
leave behind, so that you can serve
God?

_____

_____

_____

Elisha's new job of being Elijah's
helper wasn't very glamorous. But
God had called him to do it. That's
why Elisha threw himself into it
straightaway.

Wow!

Sometimes God wants
us to serve Him in the little things.
Helping out at home, doing the
cleaning at church, etc. But it's still
serving God and it still pleases Him!

Pray!

Ask God to help you turn away
from the things you wrote down.
And to enthusiastically serve Him,
especially in the less exciting jobs.

Ahab v Ben-Hadad: Round 1

23

**1 Kings
20 v 1-21**

Ahab was the evil king of Israel.

Elijah had shown him how powerful God was, but he still refused to obey the Lord.

WEIRD WORDS

Mustered
Called together

Besieged
Surrounded

Samaria
Capital of Israel

Provincial commanders
Local army leaders

Allied with him
On his side

Read 1 Kings 20 v 1-4
Cross out the wrong answers.

Ben-Hadad king of Alpen/ Aram/Arsenal gathered his entire army. Along with 32 other kings, they attacked Samaria/Samson/Salmon, the capital of Israel (v1). Ben Hadad demanded that King Ahab give him his gold, silver, women and children. King Ahab agreed/refused/ blew a raspberry.

Read verses 5-12

Ben-Hadad wasn't satisfied and told Ahab to surrender the whole city to him! (v6) This time Ahab agreed/ refused/blew a kiss (v9). So Ben-Hadad boasted that his army would turn Samaria into rust/crust/dust and destroy it (v10). Both armies prepared for battle...

Read verses 13-14

Out of the blue, a professor/ prophet/parsnip came to see King Ahab. God promised to give Ahab a mighty vegetable/victim/victory.

Read verses 15-21

King Ahab and the Israelites set out for battle while Ben-Hadad and his mates were still asleep/drunk/playing cards (v16). The young Israelite officers killed/ kicked/kissed their enemies. The Arameans ran away and Ben-Hadad escaped on hamster/heffalump/ horseback (v20).

King Ahab and the Israelites had rejected God many times. But God loved His people so much that He helped them out anyway. He wanted them to see that He was the only God (v13), so they would turn back to Him.

Pray!

Thank you, Lord, that you show us far more love and patience than we deserve. Thank you that you give us the chance to turn back to you, no matter what we've done.

Ahab v Ben-Hadad: Round 2

**1 Kings
20 v 22-30**

God gave King Ahab and the Israelites victory over Ben-Hadad and the Arameans.

But the war's not over yet...

WEIRD WORDS

Plains
Large flat area of land

Mustered
Gathered

Provisions
Food and water

Inflicted casualties
Killed people

Read 1 Kings 20 v 22

Add the vowels (aeiou) to show what the prophet said to Ahab.

Str__ngth__n y__ __r p__s__t__ __n because n__xt spr__ng, the k__ng of __r__m will __tt__ck you __g__ __n.

God was still helping and protecting the Israelites.

Read verses 23-25

What ridiculous advice did the advisers give Ben-Hadad?

Israel's g__ds are g__ds of the h__lls. So if we raise a huge __rmy and f__ght th__m on the pl__ __ns, we w__ll be str__ng__r th__n th__m.

They underestimated God and thought that He could only help the Israelites when they fought in the hills!

Think!

Do you ever underestimate God? Maybe you think God is so powerful that He couldn't possibly be interested in the puny details of your life. Wrong! God is the Lord of small things as well as the big stuff! He cares about YOU!

Read verses 26-30

God was right — the Arameans did attack Israel in the spring!

The Isr__ __l__t__ __rmy was sm__ll and looked like two tiny fl__cks of g__ __ts! But the Aramean __rmy was massive and c__v__r__d the c__ __ntrys__d__ (v27).

But God gave little Israel victory over mighty Aram. God showed that He was far more powerful than the Arameans thought. And He wanted the Israelites to know that He was the only true God.

Action!

Ever forget how great, loving and powerful God is? Look up these Bible verses: **Psalm 18 v 2, Psalm 33 v 4-5, Psalm 113 v 4-9**. Pick one and learn it, or turn it into a poster for your wall.

**1 Kings
20 v 31-34**

*God has helped
King Ahab and
the Israelites
defeat Ben-Hadad
and his huge
army.*

*But Ben-Hadad is
still alive…*

WEIRD WORDS

Merciful
Forgiving

Sackcloth
Clothes made from
horrible rough goats'
hair

Treaty
Agreement to make
peace

Off the hook

Read 1 Kings 20 v 31-34

Ben-Hadad's officials went to King
Ahab, hoping he would forgive
them. But victorious kings usually
killed or imprisoned their enemies.
So the officials wore sackcloth and
ropes to show they wanted to be
humble servants of Ahab.

*What surprising thing did Ahab say
when he heard Ben-Hadad was still
alive (v32)?*

Ahab let him off the hook! Ben-
Hadad promised to give back the
cities the Arameans had captured
from the Israelites. And then Ahab
said…

Sounds like Ahab is being
surprisingly kind and forgiving.
Surely that's the godly thing to do.
But check out what God said in
Deuteronomy 20 v 16-18.

God told them to destroy His
enemies in their land, otherwise
they would tempt the Israelites into
worshipping false gods and rejecting
the Lord. So Ahab was disobeying
God's law.

Think!

What things in your life do you
need to destroy because they
cause you to sin against God?

_____

_____

_____

Ask God to help you wipe out
these things from your life.
Where do you need to start?

B C D E F H I L M O P R S T U W Y

Prophet surprise

26

1 Kings 20 v 35-43

Yesterday we read how God had commanded the Israelites to destroy His enemies.

But King Ahab disobeyed God and let evil Ben-Hadad off the hook.

WEIRD WORDS

Talent of silver
A lot of silver — 34kg of it

Sullen
Gloomy and miserable

Read 1 Kings 20 v 35-36

Weird. This guy refused to wound the prophet, so the prophet set a lion on him! Seems unfair?

Cross out the Xs to show who really ordered the wounding.

**XBYXXTXHEXWOXXRDX
XOFXTHXEXLOXXRXDXX**

B_____

_____

_____ (v35)

The prophet was God's messenger, so this man was refusing to obey God. And he was rightly punished.

Read verses 37-40

Aha! Now we know why he wanted to be wounded. It was a disguise to help teach a lesson to King Ahab. Here's what he told Ahab…

I was told to guard a man, and if I let him escape, I would pay for it with my own life. But when I wasn't looking, he disappeared!

The solution seemed obvious to Ahab…

You have pronounced your own sentence! You will have to die for letting him escape.

But read verses 41-43

King Ahab said the prophet should die for letting his enemy escape. But Ahab himself had let God's enemy Ben-Hadad go free!

Cross out the Zs to reveal what God said to disobedient Ahab.

**YZOZUSEZTFREZEZMY
ZENZEMYSOZZYOZUZW
IZLLPAZZYFOZRIZTWIZ
ZZTHZYOZUZRLZIZFEZ**

Y_____

_____

_____

_____ (v42)

Ahab and the Israelites had disobeyed God's Word. They'd let off people who did terrible things against God.

Wow!

That's how important God's Word is! We can't just ignore it. People who ignore God and refuse to turn to Jesus will one day be punished by God.

Today we start reading an incredible book called Mark.

It's packed with miracles, top teaching, scandal, and above all... Jesus.

But first, let's pray.

PRAY

Ask God to help you understand what He wants to say to you as you read Mark.

Ask Him to help you learn loads about Jesus, so that you become more like Him.

Mark: All about Jesus

No prizes for guessing who wrote this book! But what was he writing about?

Read Mark 1 v 1 to find out

The good news...

"Gospel" means **"good news"**. Mark has things to tell us which today are still the best things anyone could hear.

...of Jesus Christ (the Messiah)

Most people switch off when they hear that name. But read the verse again — Jesus is the Son of God!!!

Do you want to know more about Jesus, the most important person in history? Then stick with Mark as he tells us all about Jesus.

Use the wordsearch to find five phrases from Mark 1 v 1. Fill them in below the wordsearch and read what they mean.

E	N	G	T	T	O	L	S	S
T	J	V	S	Y	C	U	O	E
B	E	G	I	N	N	I	N	G
F	S	O	R	O	K	F	O	Y
S	U	S	H	B	J	Z	F	R
H	S	P	C	J	P	M	G	A
A	S	W	E	N	D	O	O	G
M	E	S	S	I	A	H	D	L

B _ _ _ _ _ _ _ G

A new start. Not only the start of the book of Mark, but a new start for people who turn to God.

G _ _ _   N _ _ _

Good news worth getting excited about!

J _ _ _ _

This name means "God saves". Mark will tell us how God saves people by sending Jesus to earth.

C _ _ _ _ _ _ /
M _ _ _ _ _ _ _

These names mean God's chosen King who would rescue His people.

S_ _ O_ G_ _

God actually sent His own Son to earth! For us!

Pray!

Thank God for the great news that He sent Jesus to us.

Get the message?

**Mark
1 v 2-8**

*Would you
listen to a man
who ate insects
and wore really
weird clothes?*

*No? Then it's
probably good
you didn't
meet John the
Baptist!*

WEIRD WORDS

Prophet
God's messenger

Baptism
Dunking people
in water to show
they'd repented

Repentance
Turning away from
sin and living for
God

Thongs
Like shoelaces

Read Mark 1 v 2-3

Isaiah lived 700 years before Jesus
and was God's messenger to God's
people, the Israelites. Isaiah said that
someone would prepare the way for
Jesus. And here he is — **John the
Baptist**.

Read verses 4-5

John knew the people weren't ready
for King Jesus yet. They hadn't
been living the way God wanted
them to. *Cross out the Xs to show
what John told them to do.*

**XTUXRXNAXXWAXYFRX
OXXMSIXNAXXNDXBEX
XXBAXPXTXIXSEXDXX**

T_____
_____
_____

John baptised people in the River
Jordan. Being baptised showed they
wanted to be washed clean from all
their sins, ready to welcome King
Jesus.

Read verses 6-7

John's weird clothes and wild food
marked him out as a prophet (Elijah
and other prophets were just the
same!). That meant he was God's
messenger.

Read verse 8

What did John say about Jesus?

**IXBAXPTIXXSEYXOUWIX
XTHXWAXTEXRBXXUTX
HEWXIXLLXBAXXPTIXS
EYXXOUXWIXTHXXTHEX
HOXLYXXSPXIXRIXTXX**

I B_____
_____
_____
_____

Wow!

John baptised people on
the outside to show they had turned
away from sin. But Jesus would
actually forgive their sins. And He'd
give them the Holy Spirit to help
them live for God.

Pray!

See how great Jesus is??? Praise
Him right now. And ask Him to
help you see His greatness more
as you read through Mark.

Love from above

Mark
1 v 9-11

John the Baptist prepared the way for King Jesus to come and rescue His people.

Time for Jesus to make His entrance...

Read Mark 1 v 9

John had been baptising loads of people. But Jesus was no ordinary person.

> John baptised people who admitted they were sinful and needed to be forgiven. People who turned away from their sin.

> But Jesus had NEVER sinned. So He didn't need to repent. Jesus was baptised to obey God.
>
> It was all part of God's plan.

Next, God lets us know just how special and important Jesus is.

Read verse 10

and go back 1 letter (B=A, C=B).

U I F   T Q J S J U

D B N F   E P X O

P O   K F T V T

M J L F   B

E P W F

Jesus had the Holy Spirit in Him, helping Him to serve God, His Father. The great news is that all Christians have the Holy Spirit too, helping them to live for God!

Read verse 11

God said

" ____ ____
    Z P V   B S F

____ ____ ;
N Z   T P O

____ ____
X J U I   Z P V

__ ____ ____
J   B N   X F M M

____ "
Q M F B T F E

Jesus is God's Son, who God loves very much. Yet He sent Jesus to rescue people from their sinful ways!

Pray!

Thank God loads for sending His perfect Son, who He loves, to be your Rescuer!

**Mark
1 v 12-13**

*Mark is giving
us evidence
that Jesus is the
Christ — the
King who God
sent to rescue
His people.*

Tempting time

Read Mark 1 v 12-13

That's nearly six weeks! Do you
think you'd survive in the hot
and dangerous desert for 40 days
without any food? For Jesus it was
even worse than that.

*Unjumble the anagrams to show
who was with Jesus in the desert.*

S_____
S A N T A

That's the **devil**. Right from the
start he was trying to defeat Jesus.
Satan would try anything to stop
Jesus from rescuing His people.

W_____   A_____
L I D W   A M S N A I L

There were all sorts of creatures in
the desert that could have attacked
Jesus…

A_____
S L A N G E

…but angels looked after Him! God
protected His Son.

Jesus didn't give in to the devil's
temptations (check out Matthew 4
v 1-11 for the full story). Later on in
Mark we'll see Satan try other ways
to beat Jesus. But Satan will never
stop God's plans.

The devil tempts all of us. He wants
us to give in to sin and stop living
God's way.

Think!

In what ways does the
devil tempt YOU to do wrong?

_____

_____

_____

Don't get too down about it!
We all give in to temptation
sometimes. But it doesn't stop God
from loving us. Check out these
brilliant verses…

1 Corinthians 10 v 13
Romans 8 v 38-39

Pray!

Talk to God about your
temptations. Be honest. Ask Him
to help you fight these things.
And keep asking Him; it won't
happen overnight.

Fisherman's friend

Mark
1 v 14-20

Jesus survived 40 testing days in the desert, being tempted by the devil.

Now Jesus is back in Galilee and He's got some important things to say.

WEIRD WORDS

Galilee
The northern part of Palestine

Read Mark 1 v 14-15

THE KIN · THE GO · EAR · OD NEWS · F GOD · LIEVE · GDOM O · T AND BE · ME N · HAS CO · REPEN

Fit the white blocks together to reveal what Jesus said.

THE KIN		

Wow!

The kingdom of God isn't a place, like Wales. It's Jesus ruling over His people, wherever they live. The kingdom of God is near because Jesus the King has arrived.

*Now fit the **shaded** blocks together.*

REPEN		

Wow!

People need to REPENT (turn away from their sinful way of life) and BELIEVE the good news that Jesus can rescue them from sin. That's the only way to become part of God's kingdom.

Now read verses 16-20

Jesus changed the lives of these fishermen. *What did He say to them (v17)?*

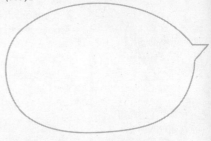

That doesn't mean catching people in large nets! It means telling people about Jesus the King, so they can start to follow Him too.

Think!

We've touched on some big questions today. Do you believe the good news about Jesus? Have you repented? Do you tell other people about Jesus?

Pray!

Talk to God about your answers.

**Mark
1 v 21-28**

*Mark is giving
us lots of
evidence that
Jesus is God's
Son.*

*Let's follow
Jesus into the
synagogue...*

WEIRD WORDS

Capernaum
Town on the edge
of the Sea of
Galilee. Jesus did
loads of miracles
there.

Sabbath
Jewish holy day
when they rested

Synagogue
Where people met
to pray and learn
from God's Word

Impure spirit
An evil spirit who
wanted to hurt the
man

Spirit-splatting stuff

Read Mark 1 v 21-22

*To find the first piece of evidence
about Jesus, take every 3rd letter
starting with the first J.*

```
J T A E H U S E T U S H S P O
T I R A R I U I T G T Y H K O T
N V W E E I W R T W E H H V
A O I U J L T E S H S P O U I R
S R I W I T A T Y S S
```

1. J_____

_____

_____

The people couldn't believe their
ears! Jesus' teaching wasn't the
same as other teachers'. His
teaching came straight from God,
His Father.

Wow!

We're so privileged. We get
to read the words of Jesus Christ!
We get teaching straight from God's
Son! So keep listening to what
He says in Mark's book.

Read verses 23-24

Impure spirits were God's enemies
and they often made people ill. But
God is far more powerful than any
impure spirit!

*Now take every 3rd letter beginning
with T.*

2. T_____

_____

_____

The impure spirit called Jesus **the
Holy One of God**. He knew that
Jesus had been sent by God, so he
was terrified.

Read verses 25-28

*Now write down every 3rd letter,
beginning with A.*

3. A_____

_____

_____

Jesus commanded the spirit to leave
the man, and it did! Jesus was in
charge. Nothing is more powerful
than Jesus!

Are you as amazed by Jesus as these
people were (v27)?

Pray!

Thank Jesus that we can read His
amazing teaching. And thank Him
that nothing is more powerful
than Him.

33

Mark
1 v 29-34

So far we've found out that Jesus is God's Son.

He is an awesome teacher who has authority over people and power over evil spirits.

And that's not all...

Fever pitch

Ever been laid up in bed with a boiling temperature? It's a rotten feeling when you're as weak as a kitten and hotter than the Sahara desert in summer.

Simon's mother-in-law had a nasty fever. Except in those days a fever was often life-threatening.

Read Mark 1 v 29-31

Fill in all the missing Es to show what happened.

> J__sus w__nt up
> to h__r, took h__r hand
> and h__lp__d h__r up.
> Th__ f__v__r l__ft h__r
> and sh__ b__gan to
> wait on th__m again.

That's incredible! Jesus healed her instantly. No one but Jesus could heal someone that quickly. In a second she was well enough to get a meal for Him and His disciples.

Unsurprisingly, a doctor like that was very popular...

Read verses 32-34

This time, fill in all the missing As and Ss.

> Je__u__ he__led
> m__ny who h__d
> v__rious di__e__ __e__.
> He __l__o drove out
> m__ny demon__.

JESUS HAS COMPLETE POWER OVER ILLNESS!

Hold on a minute! Why wouldn't Jesus let the demons tell people who He was? (v34)

Because it wasn't the right time for people to know who Jesus was — that He was the Rescuer who God had promised His people. That time would come later. God's timing is always perfect.

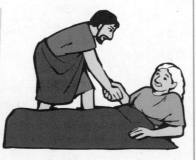

Pray!

Think of someone you know who is ill. Pray that God will help them through this time and make them better.

Rise and shine

**Mark
1 v 35-39**

Jesus must have been exhausted after such a hectic day.

First teaching in the synagogue, then healing hundreds of people after sunset.

A lie-in the next morning would have been nice!

WEIRD WORDS

Solitary place
Quiet place with no one else around

No chance of that happening!
Read Mark 1 v 35

When did Jesus get up?

It was still dark — long before sunrise. There must have been a really good reason for getting up so early. *Find it at the end of verse 35.*

To p_____

Jesus wanted to speak to God, His Father. That was much more important than sleeping in.

Think!
**How about YOU?
Do you pray at all?**

YES/NO _____

Do you just squeeze in a quick prayer when there's time?

YES/NO _____

Would you get up early to speak to God — even if you were tired?

YES/NO _____

Read verses 36-37

Action!
You're never too busy to pray! If you feel that life is hectic and there are a million things on your mind… that's exactly when you need to talk to God! Try it the next time life is crazy.

Read verse 38-39
Preaching was massively important to Jesus. He wanted to tell everyone to turn away from their sin and turn to God (v15).

Pray!

Take extra time today to TALK TO GOD. Tell Him what's on your mind. And ask Him to help you spread the good news about Jesus.

Love for a lonely leper

**Mark
1 v 40-45**

Ever been ill with something catching, like measles or chicken pox?

It can be pretty lonely when your friends keep away in case they catch it too.

WEIRD WORDS

Indignant
Angry, cross

Sacrifices that Moses commanded
The leper was to go to the temple, offer sacrifices (gifts) to God, and the priest would declare him to be cured and clean again.

LEPROSY FACT FILE

In Bible times, leprosy was a nasty, incurable disease that was easy to catch. It made your skin go all lumpy and horrible. Or even drop off.

Nobody wanted to be friends with a leper, in case they caught it too. So everyone stayed clear whenever they saw a leper coming.

But one leper got a real surprise. He met someone who didn't run away from Him.

Read Mark 1 v 40-42

Use the code to reveal what Jesus did.

__ __ __ __ __ __ __ __ __ .

No one else did.

__ __ __ __ __ __ **him.**

No one else would.

__ __ __ __ __ __ __ **him.**

No one else could.

Some Bibles translate v41 as "Jesus was indignant". But He's not cross with the man for having leprosy.

Jesus is "indignant" about the situation. He is cross that the world He made has been messed up by sin, so that now things go wrong and people get ill. Because Jesus loves this man, He is indignant about what has gone wrong — and He wants to put it right...

Jesus touched this man and cured Him! Jesus showed He had power over sickness. But there was a price to pay...

Read verses 43-45

Crowds flocked to Jesus to see more miracles. But that wasn't why Jesus came. He came to **preach** (see v38) and tell people the good news. But now He had to stay away from the towns because of the crowds.

Pray!

In some countries, like India, Brazil and Indonesia, leprosy is still a big problem. Pray for *The Leprosy Mission* and for the people they help. You can find out more at www.leprosymission.org

---

A	B	C	D	E	H	I	L	M	O	R	T	U

Dropping in

36

**Mark
2 v 1-12**

*So far, we've
seen that Jesus
has power
over people,
evil spirits, and
sickness.*

*More incredibly,
Jesus has the
power to
forgive sins
too...*

WEIRD WORDS

Paralysed
Not able to walk

Blaspheming
Claiming to be God
— a serious crime

Son of Man
Jesus

Read Mark 2 v 1-4

These guys wanted their paralysed friend to be healed. And they believed that Jesus could do it.

They were so desperate to get him to Jesus, what did they do?

[ ]

Read verse 5

What did Jesus say to the man?

[speech bubble]

The man needed to **walk**, so why did Jesus talk to him about **sin**?

Wow!

Sin is more than just doing wrong stuff. Sin is doing what we want instead of what God wants. Sin separates us from God. This man couldn't walk, but he had a far bigger problem — sin.

Jesus claimed to have the power to forgive sins! This upset some of the religious leaders...

Read verses 6-7

They couldn't believe that Jesus was claiming to have the same power as God. But Jesus **is** God, and He proved it to them.

Read verses 8-12

Which of these is easiest to say?

A Your sins are forgiven	B Get up and walk

It's easier to say **A** because no one can see if it's true or not! So, to show that He does have power to forgive sins, Jesus also said **B**!

And then He healed the man in front of everyone!

Jesus proved that He has the power to forgive sins.

Think!

Only JESUS has the power to forgive sins. Have you asked Him to forgive yours?

If you want to, tell Him you're SORRY for letting Him down. And that you want to live for Him, not yourself. Ask Him to FORGIVE you. Make sure you tell an older Christian you've asked Jesus to forgive you.

37

**Mark
2 v 13-17**

*Which of these
needs a doctor?*

Jack
*has flu and can
barely move*

Grace
*is covered in
green boils!*

Jess
*feels really really
healthy*

WEIRD WORDS

Pharisees
Religious leaders.
Most of them were
against Jesus.

Righteous
Here it means people
who thought they
were good.

Dinner with a sinner

*Go back one letter to reveal a
famous phrase.*

J U   J T

O P U   U I F

I F B M U I Z

X I P   O F F E   B

E P D U P S   C V U

U I P T F   X I P

B S F   J M M

Sounds obvious? Well it wasn't
obvious to the Jewish leaders.

Read Mark 2 v 13-16

Who did Jesus call to follow Him?

M F W J

Levi was also known as **Matthew**
(yep, the disciple who wrote the
Bible book *Matthew*). He was a tax
collector who worked for the hated
Romans.

The Pharisees were horrified
that Jesus made friends with tax
collectors and other people they
didn't respect. They thought He
should only hang out with "good"
people like them!

But what's that got to do with sick
people and doctors?

Read verse 17

I F B M U I Z

People who think they're good

J M M

People who know that they're sinful

E P D U P S

Jesus

Jesus knows that people who think
they're good enough won't ask Him
(the sin doctor) to forgive them.

But people who realise how sinful
they are will turn to Jesus for
forgiveness. And He'll cure their sin
problem!

Pray!

Pray that your non-Christian
friends will realise their need to
turn to Jesus for the cure. Ask
God to help you tell them about
Jesus, the sin doctor.

38

Fast and furious

Mark 2 v 18-22

Ever been to a wedding?

Imagine if there were no food, not even a wedding cake!

WEIRD WORDS

Disciples
Followers, students

Garment
Item of clothing

Wineskins
Wine bottles made from the skin of animals

Read Mark 2 v 18-19

The Pharisees and the followers of John the Baptist were fasting.

> **FASTING** is not eating food for a while. It was often a sign of being sad. In those days, many Jews fasted twice a week!

But there was no reason why Jesus' disciples should fast. Jesus compared Himself to a **bridegroom** (v19). His disciples were like wedding guests. They were so happy to be with Jesus (the bridegroom). Why should they be sad and go without food?!

Read verse 20

Jesus knew that He would soon die. When that happened, His followers would be incredibly sad. Then they'd fast. (Yet their sorrow wouldn't last long — God would raise Jesus back to life!)

> The message of Jesus is that He came to **RESCUE** us. He died for us so that we can be friends with God.
>
> But the Pharisees said the people had to keep a set of rules to be friends with God.
>
> The two messages don't mix!

Read verses 21-22

and draw what's missing.

You wouldn't sew a new

onto an old

or pour

into old

- If you patch up **old** clothes with **new** material, they'll rip!
- If you pour new wine into brittle old wineskins, they'll split.

If you try to fit the message of **Jesus** into a human set of rules, it won't work. The **Pharisees** said: *"You must keep our rules to please God"*. **Jesus** said: *"Repent (turn away from sin) and believe the good news"*.

You can't become a Christian by keeping rules or trying to be good. Only by **trusting Jesus** to forgive your sin.

Pray!

Thank God that you don't need to keep a set of rules to be His friend. Thank Him for sending Jesus as your Rescuer.

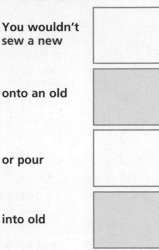

Corn on the job

**Mark
2 v 23-28**

In the Old Testament, God made a good rule: You shall not work on the Sabbath. (Exodus 20 v 10)

One day a week was set aside as a day of rest.

WEIRD WORDS

Pharisees
Religious leaders. Most of them were against Jesus.

Righteous
Here it means people who thought they were good.

But the Pharisees added loads of **extra rules** of their own. They listed 39 things you must not do on the Sabbath!

On the Sabbath...

- **DON'T walk more than 1km from your home**
- **DON'T pick any crops**
- **DON'T cook any food**
- **DON'T do anything else that we decide is work**

Read Mark 2 v 23-24

Jesus' disciples were really hungry so they picked some corn to eat. The Pharisees' rules said this was wrong because it was working on the Sabbath. (Does that sound like work to you??!)

Read verses 25-26

Jesus reminded the Pharisees what King David had done when he was starving (it's in 1 Samuel 21 v 1-6). The Pharisees would have been horrified at that, but God didn't tell David it was wrong. So it can't have been!

Read verses 27-28

and fill in the vowels (aeiou) to show what Jesus said.

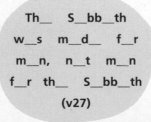

Th__ S__bb__th w__s m__d__ f__r m__n, n__t m__n f__r th__ S__bb__th
(v27)

Wow!
God made the Sabbath a special day. A day to rest from work, to chill out, and to spend more time with Him.

God **didn't** say that His people shouldn't eat, walk, cook or have fun on the Sabbath. If you keep Sunday as a day of rest, it's OK to do necessary stuff, and even do things you enjoy!

Th__ S__n __f M__n __s L__rd __v__n __f th__ S__bb__th (v28).

Jesus is Lord of the Sabbath. He's in charge of it because He is God! So we should give our rest days (as well as our work/school days) over to pleasing Him.

Pray!

Don't get hung up on religious rules. Instead pray about giving your heart to serving Jesus and pleasing Him.

Genesis: Sin spreads

**Genesis
4 v 1-8**

*Today we're
back in Genesis.*

*Adam and Eve
have disobeyed
God and
brought sin into
the world.*

*Will their kids
be any better?*

WEIRD WORDS

Offering
Gift to God

Fat portions
The best bits of
meat from Abel's
sheep

Downcast
Sad and grumpy

Read Genesis 4 v 1-5

Cain and Abel gave offerings to God
to show they worshipped Him. So
why was God only pleased with one
of them?

CAIN	ABEL
gave God an inferior gift. It wasn't good enough.	gave God the very best pieces of meat he had.

Think!

Do you give God the
very best? Do you give Him enough
of your time? Do you try your best
to live for Him? Or do you just give
Him the scraps of your life?

Read verses 6-7

God saw how upset Cain was, and
gave him some great advice.

*In the speech bubble below, put
God's advice from v7 into your own
words.*

God told Cain to deal with his anger
and sin or it would take over his life.

Read verse 8

Tragic. Cain didn't control his
anger and ended up killing his own
brother.

Sin spreads. Anger can lead to one
bad thing after another.

Own up!

Be honest and write
down some of the bad
stuff you've said, thought or done
recently.

_____

_____

_____

_____

Pray!

Say sorry to God for those things.
Ask Him to help you fight the sins
you struggle with so they don't
get a grip on your life.

44

Cain's pain

Genesis 4 v 9-26

Cain couldn't control his anger and murdered his brother Abel.

But he couldn't hide his sin from God...

Fill in the vowels as God teaches us some lessons about sin.

WEIRD WORDS

Am I my brother's keeper?
Do I look after him all the time?

Yield
Give

Vengeance
Punishment for killing Cain

1. CAIN'S PUNISHMENT
Read Genesis 4 v 9-12

Cain stupidly lied to God, pretending not to know what had happened to Abel. But God knew, and punished Cain.

He would no longer be able to grow cr__ps in the gr__ __nd. And he'd become a r__stl__ss w__nd__r__r with no h__m__ (v12).

> God hates sin and rightly punishes it.

2. GOD'S GOODNESS
Read verses 13-16

Cain thought he would be murdered. But God promised to keep him safe.

G__d put a m__rk on C__ __n so that no one would k__ll him (v15).

> Even though we let God down, He still gives us far more than we deserve.

3. SIN SPREADS
Skim through verses 17-24

God kept His word, and no one killed Cain. In fact, Cain's family grew. But they didn't learn from Cain's mistake.

L__m__ch k__ll__d a m__n for revenge and was pr__ __d about it (v23).

> Putting yourself first, instead of God, can lead to all sorts of sin.

4. GOD GIVES HOPE
Read verses 25-26

P__ __pl__ b__g__n to c__ll on the n__m__ of the L__rd.

Even with so many sinful people around, some people still lived for God! There was still hope...

Pray!

Thank God that He gives us far more than we deserve. Thank Him that even though the world is sinful, He's still with us, giving us hope.

Golden oldies

Read Genesis 5 v 1-3

When God created humans, who did He create them to be like? (v1)

[ ]

Adam was created as an image of what God is like. But Adam messed up and brought sin into the world.

So who was Adam's son Seth like? (v3)

[ ]

Wow!

Humans are created in God's image. We show a little bit of what God is like! But we're also descended from Adam, so we're like him too. That's why we're all sinful. We all disobey God sometimes.

Read verses 4-17

Unjumble the anagrams to reveal five names. Fill in how long each one lived.

_____ : _____ yrs

D A M A

_____ : _____ yrs

H E T S

_____ : _____ yrs

S H O N E

_____ : _____ yrs

N A K E N

_____

E L H A M L A L A

                    : _____ yrs

Wow, in those days people lived an incredibly long time! Yet something happened to each one of them. *What? The answer's at the end of verses 5, 8, 11, 14 & 17.*

And then he d_____

Death entered the world because of the sin of Adam and Eve. Even if we live to be 100, one day we'll die too. It's the one thing no one can avoid!

Read Romans 5 v 12

Since the beginning of time everyone has sinned, so everyone will eventually die.

But...

Read Romans 5 v 17
Death won't separate us from God for ever if we trust Jesus to rescue us!

Take it away, Enoch!

43

**Genesis
5 v 18-32**

*We're still looking
at Adam's family
tree.*

*Keep your
eyes peeled
for something
surprising…*

Read Genesis 5 v 18-32

*How many years did Methuselah live
for? (v27)*

years

That's amazing! He lived longer than
anyone else the Bible tells us about.
But that's not the big surprise.

*How old was Noah when he became
a dad? (v32)*

years

That's unbelievably old to start
looking after babies! But that's not
today's big surprise. (More about
Noah in the next few days.)

*Flick through the verses again and
spot which of these is the odd one
out.*

Jared	Enoch
Methuselah	
Lamech	Noah

The answer is in **Hebrews 11 v 5**.

Enoch never died! Instead, God
took him away to be with Him!
God saved Enoch from the awful
experience of death.

**Read Hebrews 11 v 5-6 to
find out why**

Get that? Enoch pleased God.

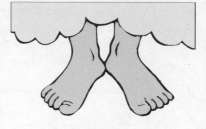

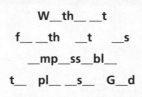

But surely it's
impossible to please
God! He's so holy and
we're so sinful.

That's true… almost.

*Fill in the blanks by finding the
words from Hebrews 11 v 6.*

**W__th__ __t
f__ __th __t __s
__mp__ss__bl__
t__ pl__ __s__ G__d**

Enoch had **FAITH**. He believed in
God, lived for Him, and trusted that
God would look after Him.

Think & pray!

Do you want to please God? First
we need faith — to trust Jesus to
rescue us from our sin. Then we
can please God! Ask God to show
you how you can please Him.

WEIRD WORDS

Labour/toil
Work

Commended
Praised

Earnestly
Seriously

Sin story

Genesis 6 v 1-7

Oh dear, people are living their own selfish ways again...

Read Genesis 6 v 1-3

The Bible doesn't explain who the *sons of God* or *daughters of humans* were. But it's obvious that they were disobeying God. So God punished them by drastically shortening people's lives.

How old was Methuselah when he died (Genesis 5 v 27)?

_____

But now humans would live until they were _____ years old (Genesis 6 v 3).

Read Genesis 6 v 4-5

People kept on sinning against God.

*Cross out the **X**s to reveal what God saw (v5).*

```
XTHXELOXRDSAXWHOXX
WWIXCKEDXXEVXERYXOX
NEONXEAXXRTHWAXSAND
XHOXWEVXXILTHXEIXXRT
HOXUXGHXXTSWERXXEX
XALXLTHXETIXMEXX
```

The_____

_____

_____

_____

_____

Put one tiny drop of ink (or paint) into a bowl of clear water. It will gradually spread out until all the water is inky coloured.

Sin's like that. Through Adam and Eve, sin entered the world. It soon spread to Cain, and to each new generation. Gradually, humans became more and more sinful.

Adam had been created in God's perfect image. But now look at his descendants! They lived only to please themselves and did all kinds of evil things. It broke God's heart.

Read verses 6-7

Think!

God loves us so much, it breaks His heart when we sin against Him. He hates sin. So God decided to wipe sinful humans off the face of the earth.

Pray!

Say sorry to God for specific times you've disobeyed Him and upset Him.

Tomorrow:
God throws Noah a lifeline!

45

**Genesis
6 v 8-13**

**THE END OF THE
WORLD?!**

*People were
sinning loads and
refusing to live
God's way.*

*So God decided
to wipe them all
out...*

WEIRD WORDS

**Righteous/
blameless**
Godly. Noah wasn't
perfect, but he lived
for the Lord.

Corrupt
Evil, sinful

Walk this way

Read Genesis 6 v 11-13

*Which word is used three times to
describe what the world was like?*

c_____

People were pleasing themselves
instead of pleasing God, who'd
created them. They disobeyed Him,
ignored Him and lived entirely for
themselves.

Action!

Do you live for yourself
or for God? Or a bit of both?

How can you live more for God?

_____

_____

_____

So God
decided
to put an end
to all people.

Well, almost
all of them.
One man
and his
family would
survive.

This was
Noah (v13).

Why would God rescue Noah?

Read verses 8-10

*and go back one letter to reveal
some facts about Noah.*

O P B I   G P V O E

G B W P V S

X J U I   U I F

M P S E   **because**

I F   X B M L F E

X J U I   H P E

Noah loved God, and lived his life
to please God. He obeyed God —
unlike everybody else.

Pray!

Ask God to help you
please Him more. Ask Him to help
you do the things you wrote down
under *Action!*

Keep praying!

Think of people you know who
refuse to live God's way. Ask the
Lord to turn their lives around so
that they live to please Him.

**Genesis
6 v 14-22**

*Disaster was
about to strike.*

*God was rightly
punishing a
sinful world.*

Ark life

A worldwide flood would destroy
everything on earth. The only ones
keeping their feet dry would be
Noah and his family!

Read Genesis 6 v 14-17

God gave Noah instructions to build
an enormous boat.

How big would it be?

_____**long**

_____**wide**

_____**high**

That's about the size of a large
ferry! And Noah had to build it!

Read verse 18

God would rescue Noah and his
family from the flood. And He
would make a **c**_____
with them.

*A COVENANT was an agreement
between God and His people. God
would promise to look after Noah
and his family. And Noah would
promise to serve God. But that all
comes later in chapter 9.*

Read verses 19-21

God didn't destroy everything He'd
created. Noah had to fill the ark
with every kind of animal and every
kind of plant used for food.

Read verse 22

God asked Noah to do some weird
things! Build a MASSIVE boat and
then fill it with animals and plants?!
Sounds crazy!

But fill in the gaps from verse 22.

**No__h d__d e__er__th__ng
j__st as __od
__omm__nd__d h__m**

Pray!

Ask God to help you follow
Noah's example. That you'll obey
God and do what He commands
us to do in the Bible.

WEIRD WORDS

Ark
Huge boat

Pitch
Black sticky, gooey
stuff used to seal
the boat and make
it water-tight

Cubit
About 45
centimetres

Covenant
Agreement

Ark and ride

Quick quiz!

*Name an animal
beginning with
each of these
letters:*

N

O

A

H

S

A

R

K

Read Genesis 7 v 1-5

God wanted to save every kind of
living thing. That's why the ark had
to be so massively huge. Elephants
and hippos, emus and tree frogs all
had to find room.

**How many
of each clean
animal? (v2)**

**How many of
each unclean
animal? (v2)**

It seems a bit strange that some
animals were called **clean** and
others **unclean**. The clean animals
(like cows and sheep) weren't better
at washing! They were animals
that could be offered to God as a
sacrifice (gift).

But how would Noah get all these
animals into his boat?

Read verses 6-10

Noah had some hard things to do
for God:

• build a humungous boat

• fill it with food for the animals
and birds

• believe that God would cause a
flood even though the sun was
shining

But God didn't tell Noah to do
anything impossible. God knew
that Noah couldn't catch all those
animals on his own.

So God made the animals come to
Noah (v 8-9)!

Read verse 5 again

Noah obeyed God by doing the
things he could do. And he trusted
God to do the rest.

Wow!

God doesn't expect us to
do impossible stuff! We can leave
that to Him.

Does it seem impossible that your
friend will become a Christian? Or
that you'll get on better with your
sister?

Then ask God to do the impossible
— He can!

Pray!

Ask God to help you obey what
He says in the Bible. And to trust
Him to do the things that seem
impossible.

Flood, wet and tears

Watch the news on TV and there is often a natural disaster somewhere in the world.

Hurricanes, tsunamis, earthquakes, volcanoes, floods...

WEIRD WORDS

Ark
Huge boat

Pitch
Black sticky, gooey stuff used to seal the boat and make it water-tight

Covenant
Agreement

But this disaster was the worst of all. It affected the whole world. Water burst from below the ground. Rain poured down from above. And the oceans covered the whole earth.

Read Genesis 7 v 11-16

The world as Noah knew it gradually disappeared beneath the rising floodwater.

Read verses 17-24

*Cross out **FLOOD** and **WATER** to reveal the tragic results.*

```
EVERFLOODYLIVINGT
HIWATERNGONTHEFA
CEOFTHEEWATERART
HWASWFLOODIPEDOUT
```

E_____

_____

_____

_____

_____

_____ (v23)

PUNISHMENT!

The people's sin had to be punished. God's perfect world had been messed up and made dirty by sin. God had to wash it clean.

RESCUE!

God kept Noah and his family safe because Noah had trusted God.

PUNISHMENT!
Read Matthew 24 v 36-41

No one knows when Jesus will come back. But when He does, people's sin will be punished. God will punish everyone who has refused to live His way.

*Now cross out **FLOOD** and **WATER** again.*

```
CHRISTJEFLOODSUSCAM
EINTOTWATERHEWORLD
TOSAVFLOODESINNERS
```

C_____

_____

_____

_____

_____ (1 Timothy 1 v 15)

RESCUE!

God sent Jesus to rescue us from punishment. Jesus will rescue everyone who turns to Him for forgiveness!

For info about how Jesus rescues us from punishment, email discover@thegoodbook.co.uk

Ararat trap

Genesis 8 v 1-14

Phone Bob

The whole earth was flooded with water.

Even the highest mountains were under the sea!

But God had promised to keep Noah safe!

I'm really forgetful. So I write stuff on the back of my hand as a reminder.

What do you do to remember things?

[blank box]

Read Genesis 8 v 1

Fill in the blanks, going forward one letter (Z=A, A=B, B=C etc).

F N C

Q D L D L A D Q D C

M N Z G

Wow!

God doesn't forget things! When God remembered Noah, it means He acted on His promise to Noah. God always keeps His promises.

Read verses 2-14 *and fit the missing verses into the timeline.*

---

months

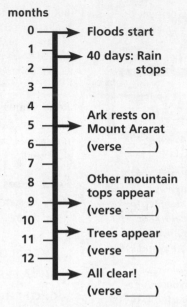

0 — Floods start

1

2 — 40 days: Rain stops

3

4

5 — Ark rests on Mount Ararat (verse ____)

6

7

8 — Other mountain tops appear

9 — (verse ____)

10

11 — Trees appear (verse ____)

12 — All clear! (verse ____)

Imagine spending over a year in a boat with all those animals. Talk about smelly and noisy!

All that time Noah trusted God to keep him safe. God had promised to look after Noah during the flood. And He kept His promise.

Think!

When you go through a difficult time, do you sometimes wonder *"Will things ever be better again?"* or *"Will God ever answer my prayer?"*

Check out Psalm 37 v 7

Pray!

Ask God to help you to trust Him patiently, as Noah did.

WEIRD WORDS

Receded
Went down

Fret
Worry

50

Genesis 8 v 15-22

Watch the news on TV and there is often a natural disaster somewhere in the world.

Hurricanes, tsunamis, earthquakes, volcanoes, floods…

WEIRD WORDS

Altar
A special table. On it, Noah cooked special animals and gave them (as a sacrifice) to God.

Burnt offerings
The animals Noah cooked and gave to God

Showing promise

But finally…

Read Genesis 8 v 15-19

How do you think Noah felt to be on dry land again?

Read verse 20

What did Noah do?

Noah cooked some of the clean animals and gave them to God. He wanted to praise and thank God for keeping him safe.

Read verses 21-22

God was pleased with Noah's offering. And He promised that He'd never destroy the earth like that again! God promised that certain things would never stop as long as the earth remains.

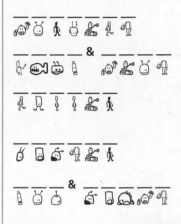

Think!

Has God kept His promise?

YES/NO _____

So can we trust God totally?

YES/NO _____

Pray!

Thank God for this great reminder that He's keeping His promises to take care of us and our world.

A B C D E F G H I L M N O R S T U V W Y

Meat to please you

*Noah and his
family were all
alone in this
strange new
world.*

*But God was with
them.*

*And He gave
them special
instructions for
living in this
changed world.*

Complete God's instructions by
reading the verses and filling in the
missing vowels (aeiou).

Read Genesis 9 v 1 and 7

1. Be fr__ __tf__l
and __ncr__ __s__ in
n__mb__r and f__ll
the __ __rth.

The world would have to be filled
with people again!

Read verses 2-3

2. __v__ryth__ng th__t
l__v__s and m__v__s
will be f__ __d for you.

People could now eat meat as well
as fruit and veg. But…

Read verse 4

3. You m__st n__t eat
m__ __t w__th its
bl__ __d st__ll in it.

They drained the blood from meat
before eating it. This showed respect
to God, who had given life to all
creatures.

Read verses 5-6

4. Wh__ __v__r sh__ds
the bl__ __d of h__m__ns,
by h__m__ns sh__ll
th__ __r bl__ __d be sh__d.

God took murder very seriously.
If an animal killed a human, that
animal would also be killed. And
if a man killed another man, the
murderer would also have his life
taken.

*Why is human life so important to
God? (Genesis 1 v 27)*

1. G__d cr__ __t__d
h__m__ns
2. H__m__ns are
m__d__ in the
__m__g__ of G__d

Wow!

We're really important to
God! He created us and we show
a little bit of what He's like. That's
why we shouldn't treat other people
badly.

Pray!

Think of people you treat badly.
Ask God to help you to be kinder
to them, remembering that He
created them.

Rainbow reminder

Genesis
9 v 8-17

Do you know all the colours of the rainbow and the order they come in?

_____

_____

_____

_____

_____

_____

_____

If you're still not sure, unravel these anagrams.

R_____   O_____
DER   RAGEON

Y_____   G_____
OWELLY   ENGER

B_____   I_____
ELBU   DINGOI

V_____
ITVOLE

Making up a stupid sentence can help you remember them. How about **R**eally **O**ld **Y**aks **G**o **B**onkers **I**n **V**enezuela?!

Try making up your own:

R_____   O_____

Y_____   G_____

B_____   I_____

V_____

Now God wants us to remember something even more important.

Read Genesis 9 v 8-11

What brilliant promise did God make to Noah? (v11) Unjumble the anagrams to find out.

N_____   A_____
REVEN   AINGA

W_____   T_____
LIWL   REETH

B___   A   F_____
EB   DOLOF

T___   D   _____
OT   REDTOYS

T_____   E_____
HET   HEART

God knew that people would still disobey Him. Yet He gave them the whole of the earth to live in and enjoy. And He promised never again to destroy the earth with a flood.

Read verses 12-17

What reminds us of God's great promise? (v16)

_____

Whenever we look at a rainbow, we can be sure that God is looking at it too, and remembering this amazing, undeserved promise He made to us.

WEIRD WORDS

Altar
A special table. On it, Noah cooked special animals and gave them (as a sacrifice) to God.

Burnt offerings
The animals Noah cooked and gave to God

Action!

Take the Rainbow Challenge! Next time you see a rainbow, tell someone why it reminds you of God's promises.

53

Another wine mess

**Genesis
9 v 18-29**

*God has been so
good to Noah,
saving him from
the flood.*

*But Noah's story
ends on a sad
note.*

Read Genesis 9 v 18-21

What did Noah do wrong?

a) he got drunk ☐

b) he ate a skunk ☐

c) he fell off his bunk ☐

What made it doubly bad?

a) he was baking ☐

b) he was faking ☐

c) he was naked ☐

Noah messed up by getting drunk.
(Ephesians 5 v 18 tells us that's
wrong.) Noah brought shame on
himself and on God too.

Wow!

Christians sometimes
mess up and disobey
God. Even godly men like Noah.
When we do mess up, we must say
sorry to God and start living His way
again.

Think!

Think of two times
you've messed up recently.

1._____

_____

_____

2._____

_____

_____

Pray!

Say sorry to God. Ask Him to
help you stop doing these things.
Thank Him that He answers our
prayers.

Read verses 22-29

What did Ham do wrong?

a) knocked the tent over ☐

b) showed great disrespect
   for his father ☐

c) finished off the wine ☐

What did Shem & Japheth do?

a) hid the wine ☐

b) hid the tent ☐

c) hid their father's shame ☐

God took Ham's sin very seriously.
He had disrespected his father
and gossipped about him, instead
of quietly covering his shame. It's
important that **we honour our
parents**.

So Ham's
descendants were
cursed. But Shem's
and Japheth's families
were **blessed**.

More about all
their descendants
tomorrow...

WEIRD WORDS

Man of the soil
Farmer

Vineyard
Where grapes for
wine are grown

Father of Canaan
Ham's descendants
became the nation of
Canaan. They were
God's enemies and
disobeyed Him.

54

**Genesis
10 v 1-32**

*Yesterday
we read how
Ham showed
disrespect to his
father, Noah.*

*God promised
to curse Ham's
descendants,
but would bless
the families of
his brothers,
Shem and
Japheth.*

WEIRD WORDS

Maritime
Living near the sea

Clans
Families

Feeling mighty?

Chapter 10 of Genesis tells us about Noah's sons Ham, Shem and Japheth and lists their descendants.

A	S	H	K	E	N	A	Z	H	C
M	R	L	U	C	J	A	V	A	N
G	D	P	E	L	E	G	T	Q	I
T	A	B	H	E	C	U	S	H	M
O	S	F	R	A	B	E	D	O	R
G	A	U	Z	V	X	L	K	G	O
A	B	A	G	T	E	A	N	E	D
R	T	R	P	U	T	M	D	T	X
M	A	A	Z	B	Y	S	K	H	P
A	H	M	J	A	G	O	M	E	R
H	A	V	I	L	A	H	W	R	A

In the wordsearch, find the names of some of Ham, Shem and Japheth's descendants (they are all in Genesis chapter 10).

JAPHETH'S DESCENDANTS

G_____

J_____

T_____

A_____

T_____

HAM'S DESCENDANTS

C_____, P_____

H_____

S_____

N_____

SHEM'S DESCENDANTS

E_____, U_____

A_____

G_____

P_____

That's a lot of people in Noah's family! Let's look at just one of them.

Read Genesis 10 v 8-9

Nimrod is described as a "mighty hunter before the Lord". He served God in what he did.

You're probably not a mighty hunter! But you can still serve God in what you do.

Action!

Describe yourself in a few words. For example "guitarist" or "tennis player". Now stick it in the space below.

I'm a mighty _____

_____

before the Lord!

Pray!

Ask God to help you serve Him in the things you do. To make you a mighty _____
_____ for Him!

55

**Genesis
11 v 1-9**

What's the biggest thing you've ever built?

Maybe something at school? Or a huge sandcastle?

_____

_____

_____

_____

WEIRD WORDS

Plain
Huge, flat area of land

Bitumen
Black gooey stuff

Mortar
Stuff for sticking bricks together

Babel babble

The people in today's passage planned to build something huge and impressive…

Genesis 11 v 1-4

What did they plan to build? To find out, fill in the missing first letters of some of the words.

__et us __uild __urselves a __ity with a __ower that __eaches to the __eavens (v4)

Why did they want to build such a tall tower?

So that we __ake a __ame for __urselves and are not __cattered over the __ace of the __arth (v4)

These people thought they were more important than God. They wanted to build an awesome tower to show just how great they were. They wanted to run their own lives, not live for God.

Think!

In what ways do you put yourself first, rather than God? Maybe you don't give God much of your time? Or you boast about stuff you've done, rather than giving God the glory?

_____

_____

_____

_____

Read verses 5-9

God saw how self-centred the people were. He made them all speak different languages, so they could no longer communicate! And He scattered them around the world.

Wow!

God is incredibly powerful and He's in control. He hates it when we turn against Him and live only to please ourselves.

Pray!

Say sorry to God for the times you put yourself first and forget about Him. Ask Him to help you be less self-centred and more God-centred.

More from Genesis next issue!

Elijah: Fiery prophet

**1 Kings
21 v 1-4**

Time to get back to 1 Kings to find out what Elijah and King Ahab are getting up to.

For a recap of what 1 & 2 Kings are about, flip back to Day 12.

WEIRD WORDS

Vineyard
Where the grapes for wine are grown

Jezreelite
From the town of Jezreel

Samaria
The main city in Israel

Sullen
Sulky

Who's who in 1 Kings

Ahab was the evil king of the Israelites, God's special people. He got people to worship Baal instead of God.

Jezebel was Ahab's wife. A nasty piece of work who killed loads of God's prophets.

Elijah the prophet spoke God's word to the Israelites. He stood up to Ahab, who wanted him dead.

Naboth was, er, let's find out…

Read 1 Kings 21 v 1-4

Ahab liked the look of Naboth's vineyard. He fancied planting some veggies there because it was right next to his palace.

But what did Naboth say to him? Cross out the Js, Ks and Ps.

T	J	O	R	D	K	B	I	D	P
H	E	L	J	F	O	R	K	T	H
P	J	K	P	J	K	P	K	J	A
A	N	C	P	C	E	S	J	I	T
T	K	E	P	N	J	T	K	S	P
I	J	O	K	A	P	O	J	H	O
R	K	F	M	Y	K	R	S	P	U
E	J	K	P	P	J	K	P	D	L
H	N	I	J	U	O	Y	K	G	P
J	K	E	H	T	P	E	V	I	J

The _____

_____

_____

_____

God had given the land of Israel (Canaan) to His people. God Himself had given this land to Naboth's family. No wonder he didn't want to give it up!

Think!

What has God given you? (Add your own)

A loving family ☐

The Bible ☐

Christian friends ☐

His Son Jesus ☐

_____ ☐

_____ ☐

_____ ☐

Do you thank God for what He's given you? Do you treat it as seriously as Naboth did?
Or are you always unsatisfied and looking for more, like Ahab?

Pray!

Thank God for the things in your list. Ask Him to help you to be grateful for all that He's given you.

51

**1 Kings
21 v 5-16**

It's not fair!

King Ahab is sulking because Naboth won't give him his vineyard.

Use the wordsearch to find today's missing words.

Stop thief!

```
S Q E F A S T I N G
O C A B H T G P F K
N T O K L O A H A B
Y H Q U R N L Z F O
J Z V I N E Y A R D
T A Y S J D X U C C
K D N R S V R R P I
I S A A D M U E B T
N X J E Z E B E L Y
G O D L E G C M V S
```

Read 1 Kings 21 v 5-7

Ahab's wife J_____
teased him for being
so pathetic.
**"Is this how you act as
k_____ of I_____?
I'll get you Naboth's
v_____."**

Ahab was the king of the Israelites, God's people. That meant he should obey God's rules. That's why he didn't just steal the vineyard. But Jezebel pressured him to ignore God and do exactly what he wanted.

Read verses 8-16

Jezebel arranged a day of
f_____ in Naboth's
c_____. She got two
s_____ to claim
that Naboth had cursed
both G_____ and King
A_____. So Naboth was
s_____ to death.

That was totally unfair. But God's people (Christians) should expect unfairness when they're serving God. In the New Testament, Peter says…

Don't be surprised at the painful trial you're suffering. But rejoice that you participate in the sufferings of Christ!

Wow!
Christians will get a hard
time for standing up for their beliefs. But they're suffering alongside Jesus! He was falsely accused, beaten and then murdered. They are suffering with Jesus and for Jesus. And that's a great privilege!

Pray!

Heavenly Father, it's amazing that Jesus suffered so much for me. Help me to stand up for Him and to cope with being treated unfairly.

WEIRD WORDS

Sullen
Sulking

Elders and nobles
Important men in the city

Fasting
Going without food for God

Scoundrels
Bad men

Bring charges
Make accusations

God nabs Ahab

**1 Kings
21 v 17-29**

*Would evil Ahab
and Jezebel
get away with
killing Naboth
and taking his
vineyard?*

No chance!

WEIRD WORDS

Devour
Eat

Vilest
Worst

Idols
Fake gods

Sackcloth
Uncomfortable
clothes worn when
upset

Meekly
Humbly, no longer
putting himself first

Read 1 Kings 21 v 17-19

God sent His messenger Elijah to tell
Ahab that God would punish him.
He would die just as Naboth had.

Wow!

God's in charge! That's
an important thing to remember
when you're hassled for being a
Christian. In the end, it is God who's
in control. One day He'll reward
those who serve Him and punish His
enemies.

Read verses 20-26

Check out the speech bubbles. *Tick
the things God did say and cross out
what He didn't say.*

> **You've done
> evil in the eyes of
> the Lord**

> **But I'll let you
> off the hook**

> **I will
> bring disaster on
> you, as I did with evil kings
> Jeroboam and Baasha**

> **I'll punish your
> descendants**

> **I'll give Jezebel a
> pet dog**

> **Jezebel will be
> eaten by dogs**

Ahab had got the people to worship
idols instead of God. He was the
most evil king Israel had ever had.
It seemed as though he would get
away with it, but...

Wow!

God doesn't let sin go
unpunished, even though it seems
like it sometimes. In the end God
will punish everyone who has
rejected Him. He'll punish everyone
who has persecuted His people. God
looks after His children!

Read verses 27-29

Amazingly, King Ahab was touched
by God's words. So God showed
incredible kindness to him by
delaying the punishment of Ahab's
family.

But Ahab still didn't turn away from
his wicked ways, so God would still
punish his family.

Pray!

Thank God that...
• He's in control.
• He's totally fair.
• He doesn't let sin go
  unpunished.
• He looks after His children,
  Christians.

2 kings in 1 Kings

1 Kings 22 v 1-9

God's people, the Israelites, had split into two kingdoms: Israel and Judah.

Israel was ruled by evil King Ahab, and Judah was ruled by godly King Jehoshaphat.

WEIRD WORDS

Aram
Israel's enemy

Ramoth Gilead
City stolen from the Israelites by Aram

Counsel
Advice

Refrain
Not do it

Read 1 Kings 22 v 1-9

Ahab wanted to invade Ramoth Gilead and asked Jehoshaphat's help. *To find out how the two kings compared, go back 1 letter.*

King Ahab

E J E O U   U V S O
,

U P   H P E

Ahab wanted what was best for himself and didn't bother asking God (v3).

B T L F E   G B L F

Q S P Q I F U T

He didn't really care what God thought. That's why his prophets only told him what he wanted to hear (v6).

I B U F E   H P E T
,

Q S P Q I F U

God's messenger always told him the truth. And the truth is sometimes unpleasant to hear, especially when you're disobeying God.

Are you like Ahab? Do you only listen to God's word (the Bible) when it suits you? Do you live to please **God** or **yourself**?

King Jehoshaphat

X B O U F E   U P

Q M F B T F   H P E

Jehoshaphat insisted on asking God if invading Ramoth Gilead was the right thing to do (v5, 7).

T U P P E   V Q

U P   B I B C

Ahab dissed God's prophet but Jehoshaphat stood up to Ahab.

Action!

That's more like it! It's much better to try and please God than ourselves. And to stand up to people when they speak against God or His people. Will you try it?

Pray!

If you really mean it, tell God that you want to please Him with what you do this week. Ask Him to help you out.

Under pressure

Find it hard talking to people about God?

Scared by the idea of standing up to people?

Then take some tips from Micaiah...

WEIRD WORDS

Threshing-floor
Important place in the city

Gore
Wound, like a bull with its horns

Multitude of heaven
Loads of angels and spirits

Deceiving
Lying

Decreed
Commanded

Read **1 Kings 22 v 9-14** *and fill in the missing first letters of words.*

__edekiah wore iron __orns and said that Ahab's army would __estroy the __rameans (v11). All the other __rophets agreed that Ahab should attack __amoth __ilead (v12). The king's messenger told Micaiah to agree with them. But Micaiah said "I can __ell him only what the __ord __ells me!" (v14)

Wow!

Micaiah faced 400 prophets, but he stuck with what God had told him. It takes guts, but we must always say what God's word (the Bible) says. That might mean speaking out against lying, or about sex before marriage. It might mean facing angry opposition. But God's word must come first.

Read verses 15-23

Micaiah made fun of Ahab, pretending to agree with the other __rophets (v15). Then he spoke God's message. The Israelites would be like __heep without a __hepherd because their king, Ahab, would be killed in battle.

Micaiah said the other __rophets had a __eceiving __pirit in them. That's why none of them spoke the truth.

Read verses 24-28

__edekiah __lapped Micaiah's __ace and called him a liar. But they would find out who was really lying when Ahab was killed and the prophets all hid. Ahab threw __icaiah into __rison (v27).

Wow!

Even as a prisoner, Micaiah still stuck with God's message! And if you want to be true to the Bible, then sometimes you will have to speak truths that people don't like.

Pray!

Ask God to give you the courage and ability to speak truth from the Bible with your friends this week.

Gone to the dogs

**1 Kings
22 v 29-40**

*King Ahab
ignored what
God's prophet
had told him, and
invaded Ramoth
Gilead anyway.*

The idiot.

WEIRD WORDS

Decreed
Commanded

King of Israel
Ahab

King of Aram
The enemy

Prostitute
Woman who is paid
for sex

**Book of the
annals of the
kings of Israel**
History book of all
the kings of Israel

*What had Micaiah said to Ahab?
(1 Kings 22 v 23)*

_ _ _ _ _ _ _ _ _ _ _ _ _

_ _ _ _ _ _ _ _ _ _

_ _ _ _ _ _ _ _ _ _ _ _ _

_ _ _ _ _ _ _ _

But read 1 Kings 22 v 29-33

The enemy couldn't find Ahab
because he was in disguise. Maybe
God was wrong and Ahab would
escape death…

Read verses 34-36

A random shot hit Ahab in the
chest! Micaiah's prophecy came
true. Nothing can stop God's plans!

*What had Elijah said about Ahab?
(1 Kings 21 v 19)*

_ _ _ _ _ _ _ _ _ _ _

_ _ _ _ _ _ _ _ _ _

_ _ _ _ _ _ _ _ _ _ _ _

Yuck! Disgusting!

Read verses 37-40

It actually came true. God's
messenger had got it right. God
rightly punished Ahab for sinning
against Him. Without God, Ahab
was only fit to feed dogs.

Wow!

God's word always comes
true. So check out these verses:

John 3 v 16-18

1 Thessalonians 4 v 16-18

God's word always comes true!

Pray!

Thank God that His word always
comes true. Thank Him for those
promises you've just read about.
What do they make you want to
say to God?

A	B	C	D	E	F	G	H	I	K	L	O	P	R	S	T	U	W	Y

Good king, bad king

**1 Kings
22 v 41-50**

*Ahab, the evil
king of Israel, is
finally dead.*

*But what about
his friend, King
Jehoshaphat?*

WEIRD WORDS

High places
Where idols were
worshipped

Sacrifices
Gifts of animals or
crops

Incense
Powder burnt to
make a sweet smell

Military exploits
Battles

Ophir
Area where gold
was mined

Remember, the Israelites had split
into two kingdoms — Israel and
Judah. Jehoshaphat was king of
Judah. Let's see if he was any better
than Ahab…

Read 1 Kings 22 v 41-50

*Fill in the vowels (aeiou) to show
Jehoshaphat's good side.*

Good stuff

**1. He f__ll__w__d the w__ys
of his f__th__r (v43)**

He followed his dad's good example
and served God.

**2. He did what was r__ght in
the eyes of the L__rd (v43)**

Unlike Ahab, Jehoshaphat didn't
turn away from God. He tried to live
God's way.

**3. He got rid of all the
pr__st__t__t__s (v46)**

These people were involved in
worshipping idols by sinning
sexually.

So Jehoshaphat served God. But
how did he **compromise** his
beliefs? How did he let God down?

Ahab | Jehoshaphat

Bad stuff

**1. He didn't r__m__v__
the h__gh pl__c__s (v43)**

Jehoshaphat didn't completely
destroy the places where idols used
to be worshipped.

**2. He made p__ __c__ with
the k__ng of __sr__ __l
(v44)**

Both Ahab and his son Ahaziah
rejected God. They sinned against
him and worshipped Baal.
Jehoshaphat should have had
nothing to do with them.

Even if we've given our lives to God,
we still **compromise** sometimes.
We do stuff we shouldn't. Maybe
keeping quiet when friends say
stuff they shouldn't. Or joining in
with the crowd when we know it's
wrong.

Think!

Can you think of any
examples in your life?

_____

_____

_____

Pray!

Say sorry to God for times you've
let Him down. Ask Him to help
you serve Him in your daily life
and not compromise.

63

Like father, like son

Remember how evil King Ahab was?

Like father, like son...

Read 1 Kings 22 v 51-52

Who did Ahaziah take after? (v52)

1. His f_____

That's Ahab. He was a very evil king of Israel.

He built a temple for the fake god Baal, and sinned against God loads.

2. His m_____

That's Jezebel. She worshipped Baal too. She also murdered Naboth and many of God's prophets.

3. J_____ son of N_____

An earlier king of Israel who stopped people worshipping God. He got them to worship golden cows instead.

Like these people, Ahaziah sinned against God, so…

Read verse 53

…God was furious with Ahaziah.

Wow!

God hates sin. It angers Him. And He punishes anyone who refuses to obey Him.

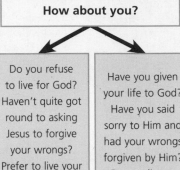

How about you?

Do you refuse to live for God? Haven't quite got round to asking Jesus to forgive your wrongs? Prefer to live your own way instead of God's way?

Have you given your life to God? Have you said sorry to Him and had your wrongs forgiven by Him? Do you live to serve God?

Read Acts 10v42

One day Jesus will return to judge everyone who has ever lived. Anyone who hasn't turned to Him for forgiveness will be punished in hell.

Read Acts 10v43

Jesus has made it possible for you to have your sins forgiven! You will never be punished for your wrongs. They're all forgiven!

Pray!

Time to talk to God. You either need to say sorry to Him and ask Him to forgive you, or you've got loads to thank God for. Go on then, do it!

Over the next few days we'll read how God punished Ahaziah.

64

**2 Kings
1 v 1-8**

Today we begin reading the book of 2 Kings.

It continues the history of God's people (the Israelites) and the kings who ruled them.

Fall guy

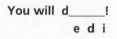

Yesterday we read that evil King Ahaziah angered God. Here's how he did it.

Read 2 Kings 1 v 1-2

Ouch! The king fell from his room, getting badly injured. *Unjumble the anagrams to show what he did next.*

Sent messengers to ask

the fake god B_____ –
a l B a

Z_____ in E_____
b u Z b e   k r o n E

if he would ever recover.

The king of God's people turned to a useless idol for help! No wonder God was furious!

Read verses 3-4
Before they got to Ekron, who did the messengers meet?

E_____
h E j a i l

What did Elijah say would happen to King Ahaziah?

You will d_____!
e d i

Read verses 5-8

Ahaziah would die because he rejected God and worshipped Baal-Zebub instead. God won't share us with other gods. He hates it when other things are more important to us than Him.

Think!

What takes up more of your life than God does? Sport? Family? Music? Be honest!

_____

_____

_____

Only pray this prayer to God if you truly mean it…

Pray!

Dear God, I'm sorry that

_____

is sometimes more important to me than you are.

Help me to put you first in my life so that I worship only you.

You're fired!

**2 Kings
1 v 9-12**

*King Ahaziah fell
from his roof,
injured himself,
then turned to
a false god for
help.*

*Elijah told him
that he would die
for rejecting God.*

So Ahaziah sent 50 soldiers to capture Elijah. He thought he could persuade Elijah to reverse the curse against him.

Read 2 Kings 1 v 9-10

God was the real King of the Israelites. He was in charge. So Ahaziah should have served God and turned to Him for help. Instead, he thought he could boss God and His prophet around.

So God showed who was really in charge by destroying the captain and his men. No one can order God around!

Wow!

It's easy to put ourselves first. Without realising it, we're making ourselves more important than God. But we should be seeking to live God's way, remembering that He's our King.

Read verses 11-12

Unbelievable! The king sent another 50 men to capture Elijah. Unsurprisingly, God destroyed them as well. Ahaziah hadn't learned his lesson.

Think!

Got a sin you keep repeating? You think you should have it under control by now, but you end up making the same mistake again and again.

What sin do you struggle with?

_____

_____

_____

Action!

1. Find a Bible verse about your problem sin *
   (eg: If it's disobeying your parents, Exodus 20 v 12; if it's lying, Proverbs 12 v 22)
2. Write it out and learn it. It really helps to have God's word on your mind.
3. Pray about it. Ask God to help you fight this sin. And keep praying about it.

No better time to start than now…

** Can't find a Bible verse? Email
discover@thegoodbook.co.uk*

Bow, wow!

**2 Kings
1 v 13-18**

Ahaziah turned
to the false god,
Baal-Zebub,
instead of God.

Elijah told
Ahaziah that he
would die for
rejecting God.

Ahaziah sent
loads of soldiers
to arrest
Elijah, but God
destroyed them
with fire from
heaven.

WEIRD WORDS

Joram
Ahaziah's younger
brother

Guess what Ahaziah did next!

a) Turned back to God ☐

b) Rejected Baal-Zebub ☐

c) Sent another 50 soldiers ☐

Read 2 Kings 1 v 13-15

What an idiot!. Ahaziah sent more
soldiers to get Elijah!

*But what was different about this
army captain?*

a) He had 51 men ☐

b) He showed respect for Elijah ☐

c) He had a fire extinguisher ☐

He knew that Elijah was God's
messenger. So he fell on his knees
and begged Elijah not to kill him
and his men.

What did the angel tell Elijah?

a) Go with the captain ☐

b) Zap him with fire ☐

c) Steal his fire extinguisher ☐

Wow!

Yesterday we saw how
God punishes those who reject
Him. But here we see God's loving
kindness. This captain bowed down
before God, so God let him off the
hook and sent Elijah back with him.

Read verses 16-18

God had told Ahaziah that he would
die for turning to another god.
God's promise came true.

Since King David died 120 years
earlier, there had been 10 kings
of Israel. *How many of them had
served God?*

10 ☐   8 ☐   6 ☐

4 ☐   2 ☐   0 ☐

The answer is none. Not one! God
had made a **covenant** with His
people — He promised to give them
a great life if they obeyed His law.
But the Israelites and their kings
rejected God and refused to serve
Him.

Pray!

Will you bow down to God right
now, as the captain did? Will you
say SORRY for the times you've
refused to obey Him?

Journey into history

God is soon going to take His prophet Elijah up to heaven.

But first, a road trip...

Elisha was with Elijah (confusing, eh?). Elisha would become God's special messenger when Elijah went up to heaven.

Read 2 Kings 2 v 1-3

Elisha insisted on travelling with Elijah as they visited different places. All of these places had played a part in the history of the Israelites.

G_____ (v1)

This was the first place the Israelites camped when they entered Canaan— the land God had promised them.

B_____ (v2)

This is where Jacob dreamed of a staircase from heaven. God promised to protect Jacob and to give Canaan to Jacob's descendants, the Israelites (Genesis 28 v 10-22).

WEIRD WORDS

Company of the prophets
Group of men who served God

Read verses 4-5

J_____ (v4)

The first city that Joshua and the Israelites captured in Canaan! (Joshua chapter 6)

Read verses 6-8

The J_____ (v6)

The main river in the country. Joshua led the Israelites into Canaan across the river Jordan (Joshua chapter 3).

God parted the River Jordan for Elijah and Elisha, just as He had parted the Red Sea so Moses and the Israelites could escape the Egyptians.

Wow!

Maybe by visiting all these important places, God is showing His people how important Elijah is. He is God's special messenger who told the Israelites to turn back to God and start living for Him again.

Pray!

Thank God for teaching us (through Elijah) to turn back to Him and to work hard at living for Him.

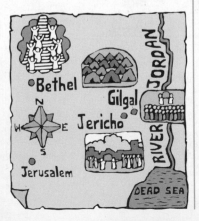

Bethel

Gilgal

Jericho

Jerusalem

RIVER JORDAN

DEAD SEA

68

**2 Kings
2 v 9-10**

Joel's dad runs a company that sells cute cuddly toys.

But his dad is getting too old and crumbly to run the business.

So he hands over the running of the business to Joel.

Joel is super excited!

Over to you, Elisha

Joel wants to take over running the business. It is his inheritance. Believe it or not, Elisha asked Elijah for a similar thing…

Read 2 Kings 2 v 9

Okay, so no cuddly toys involved. But what did Elisha ask for?

Go back one letter to find out.

B EPVCMF

QPSUJPO

PG ZPVS

TQJSJU

He wanted to carry on Elijah's work after Elijah was gone. He wanted to be God's new messenger to the Israelites.

Action!

Do you want to serve God? You may not be a prophet, but what can you do for God? (Help out with Sunday School, tell friends about Jesus?)

_____

_____

_____

Read verse 10

That's a strange answer from Elijah. Here's what he was saying.

JUT VQ

UP HPE

God would decide how Elisha could serve Him best. God chooses how we serve Him too.

Pray!

Ask God if what you've written down is the best way you can serve Him. Ask Him to help you really involve yourself in doing those things for Him.

What are you waiting for? You'd best get started doing it!

Chariot of fire

**2 Kings
2 v 11-18**

Ever seen a plane take off?

Or a helicopter?

What about a man? Ever seen one fly off into the sky???

Read 2 Kings 2 v 11-12

What a sight! A fiery chariot and horses took Elijah up to heaven in a whirlwind. He must have really pleased God. What an honour!

Remember what Elisha asked for yesterday? *Go **forward** 2 letters to find out (A=C, B=D, C=E, Y=A).*

__ __   __ __ __ __ __
R M   A Y P P W

__ __   __ __ __ __ __ __ __ ,
M L   C J G H Y F Q

__ __ __ __
U M P I

Read verses 13-15

God gave Elisha 3 signs that He'd given Elisha what he asked for.

1. __ __ __ __ __ __ __ , __ __
   C J G H Y F Q

__ __ __ __ __
A J M Y I

Elisha picked up Elijah's cloak to show that he was carrying on Elijah's work as prophet.

2. __ __ __ __ __ __ __ , __ __
   C J G H Y F Q

__ __ __ __ __ __ __
K G P Y A J C

God miraculously parted the river for him to cross. Just as He had done for Elijah (v8, 14).

3. __ __ __ __ __ __ __ __
   N P M N F C R Q

The prophets said that Elijah's spirit was resting on Elisha.

Think!

God really did want Elisha to be His new prophet. What about you? Yesterday, how did you say you'd serve God? Has God answered your prayer yet?

Read verses 16-18

The prophets didn't really believe that Elijah had gone to heaven, so they looked for him. What about you? Do you really believe that God can use **YOU** to serve Him? Or are you looking for other answers, like these prophets?

Pray!

Thank God that He wants to use you as His servant. Ask Him again to help you do what you wrote down yesterday.

Mark: All about Jesus

**Mark
3 v 1-6**

Last time we were reading Mark's book, Jesus was being hassled by the Pharisees for picking corn on the Sabbath (Jewish holy day).

Get ready for more of the same...

WEIRD WORDS

Stubborn hearts
They refused to believe Jesus was God's Son

Herodians
Supporters of King Herod, who the Pharisees didn't normally get along with

---

Make a quick list of things your hands allow you to do.

_____

_____

_____

Read Mark 3 v 1-2

This man had a shrivelled hand, making it hard for him to do things. Jesus cared for him and wanted to heal him. But the Pharisees said it was wrong to heal an injury on the Sabbath.

Read verses 3-5

Jesus could have waited until the next day to heal the man — but He didn't. *To find out why, follow the spiral to reveal Jesus' words.*

WHICH IS LAWFUL ON THE SABBATH? TO SAVE LIFE OR TO KILL? TO DO EVIL OR TO DO GOOD

_____

_____

_____

_____

It's always right to do good on the Sabbath. So Jesus healed the man.

Action!

Sometimes we make excuses for not helping people. But Jesus encourages us to do good. What can you do to help out someone in your family?

_____

_____

_____

Read verse 6

The Pharisees did evil on the Sabbath! They hated Jesus so much they got together with their enemies to plan His murder.

Wow!

What Jesus did was good and right. But His enemies hated Him for it. If we do what's good and right, we might sometimes be hated too.

Pray!

Ask God to help you do what you wrote in the action box. Ask Him to help you put up with any hassle you get.

71

Mark 3 v 7-19

Who is Jesus?

The Pharisees saw Jesus as an enemy to be killed.

Other people thought He was just a great healer...

Who is Jesus?

Read Mark 3 v 7-12

Loads of people had heard about Jesus' amazing miracles. They wanted to see Him and touch Him and be healed by Him.

On the map, draw arrows from where people travelled to see Jesus at the Sea of Galilee.

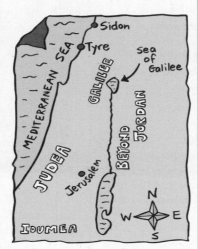

Who did the impure spirits say Jesus was? (v11)

They were right! But Jesus wouldn't let them tell the crowds who He was. He knew they wouldn't understand and it might make life difficult for Him.

Next, Jesus chose His twelve closest followers.

Read verses 13-19 *and unjumble their names.*

RETEP	P_____
SAJEM	J_____
HONJ	J_____
DRAWEN	A_____
LIPPHI	P_____
OHMELTABROW	
	B_____
THEMWAT	M_____
SATHOM	T_____
MEJAS	J_____
UTSADHEAD	
	T_____
MONIS	S_____
SAJUD	J_____

Jesus chose these men to be with Him, training them to teach others about God (v14). After He died, it would be their job to spread the great news about Him.

Wow!

All Christians are followers of Jesus! He loves them and cares for them. And He wants them to tell other people about Him.

Pray!

Praise Jesus for being the Son of God! If you're a Christian, thank Him for being your friend. Ask Him to train you to tell people about Him.

WEIRD WORDS

Galilee
The area where Jesus grew up

Apostles
It means: "those who were sent". Jesus would send out these 12 men to tell people about Him.

Speak of the devil

**Mark
3 v 20-26**

*People were
trying to work
out who Jesus
was.*

*Even though
they'd seen His
miracles, they still
wouldn't believe
He was God's Son.*

WEIRD WORDS

**Teachers of the
law**
Experts on the
Scripture (Old
Testament)

Beelzebul
The devil

Parables
Explaining things
using stories

Opposes
Fights against

Read Mark 3 v 20-21

*What did Jesus' own family say
about Him?*

They couldn't understand why He
was travelling around preaching
and healing people. They didn't
realise who He was and that He was
serving God, His real Father.

Wow!

People will sometimes
react like that to us for
following Jesus. They won't believe
He is God's Son. And they'll think
we're mad for following Him.

Read verse 22

*Who did the religious leaders say
Jesus was serving?*

B_____

That's Satan, the devil! They said
Jesus was on the devil's side! They
said that's why He had power to
drive out demons.

Read verses 23-26 for Jesus'
reply

If I was on Satan's side,
I wouldn't defeat His demons!
It'd be like a kingdom fighting
against its own soldiers! Or a
family falling apart because it
divided into groups that fought
each other! Ridiculous!

These people refused to believe that
Jesus was God's Son. So they made
up lies about Him. But Jesus showed
how stupid their claims were.

Today, many people refuse to trust
Jesus. They might even say nasty
things about Him. Or say horrible,
hurtful things to us.

Pray!

Ask God to help you to stand up
for Jesus. Even when friends or
family give you a hard time.

Ask God to help you keep your
cool, put up with hurtful words,
and never give up!

Devil defeated!

**Mark
3 v 27-30**

*The religious
leaders accused
Jesus of working
for the devil!*

*But they've
completely missed
the point...*

WEIRD WORDS

Parable
Story used by Jesus
to explain a BIG
TRUTH

Plunder
Steal

Slander
Saying bad and
untrue things

Utter
Say

Blasphemes
Speaking against
God

Read Mark 3 v 27

*Use the word pool to fill in the gaps
and show what Jesus' parable means.*

> strong   sins   No one
> Blasphemy   first   demons
> people   forgive   Spirit
> Jesus   plunder   devil
> Holy   ties   defeated

PARABLE

N_____ can break
into a s_____
man's house unless he
t_____ up the strong man
f_____. Then he can
p_____ the house.

MEANING

J_____ wouldn't have
been able to drive out the
devil's d_____ from
p_____ unless He'd
already d_____
the d_____!

Wow!

Jesus beat the devil when
He was tempted in the desert (Luke
4 v 1-13). Later, Jesus died on the
cross for us and was raised back to
life, defeating the devil for ever! If
you're a Christian, Jesus has taken
you from the devil's control!

Read verses 28-30

Jesus has the power to
f_____ our s_____ if
we turn to Him. But which
sin won't be forgiven? (v29)
B_____ against
the H_____ S_____.

That means **rejecting Jesus**. The
Holy Spirit shows us that we're sinful
and need Jesus to forgive us. People
who ignore this, and refuse to turn
to Jesus, won't be forgiven by God.

**DON'T WORRY that you
might have committed this
unforgivable sin! If you've
turned to Jesus for forgiveness,
then you can't reject Him! You're
safe with Him for ever!**

Pray!

Thank God that if we turn to
Jesus and trust Him, He will
forgive us for all the wrong stuff
we've ever done!

My family

Mark 3 v 31-35

Who's in your family? Make a list below.

_____

_____

_____

_____

_____

_____

_____

_____

Jesus' family had come to see Him. But Jesus said something surprising…

Read Mark 3 v 31-34

Jesus was in the middle of a crowd. *Reveal what He said about them (v34) by joining up the people below in the right order.*

HERE

BROTHERS

ARE

MY

MOTHER

MY

AND

Hold on! How can the crowd be Jesus' mother and brothers?!

And the people you've just joined up could also be part of the same family! They have different colour skin, speak different languages and live in different countries — yet they could all belong to the same family. **They could all have God as their Father.**

Wow!

Everyone who has God as their Father is in the same family. All believers are in the same family as Jesus!

So who's in this special family?

Read verse 35

> **Whoever_____**
> _____
> _____
> _____
> _____

Doing God's will is…

a) turning away from sinning against God ☐

b) trusting in Jesus ☐

c) living for God instead of living for ourselves ☐

d) all of these things! ☐

Answer: d

Think!

Do you live for God?

So is God your Father?

YES? Then thank Him loads!

NO? Ask God to make you one of His children.

Mark 4 v 1-12

Jesus often used stories (called parables) to explain BIG TRUTHS about Himself, His Father, and living for God.

Ear ear!

Read Mark 4 v 1-9

I wonder how many of the people drifted off and never thought any more about the story. But Jesus wanted them (and us) to ask…

What does it *mean*?

Rearrange the word blocks to form Jesus' great piece of advice from v9.

EARS	HAS	TO
WHOEVER	LET	HEAR
HEAR	THEM	

WHOEVER		

In other words, **listen** and **think** about what Jesus says.

Action!

Have you thought about what Jesus' story means? If not, do that right now. Why not write down your ideas?

Don't worry if you don't fully understand the story — most of the crowd listening to Jesus didn't get it! (We'll look at Jesus' explanation tomorrow.)

What can we do when we don't understand the Bible?

---

1. **Ask God to help us**
2. **Find someone who can explain it to us**

Read verses 10-12

*So why did Jesus teach using parables? Tick the answers you think are **true**.*

To lose the interest of those who weren't really bothered ☐

To get people thinking about the meaning ☐

To make people come to Him for an explanation ☐

All of those things! The last thing many of the people wanted was to change their ways and live for God. It was no use explaining the truth to them — they weren't interested. Jesus wanted to teach people who really wanted to understand His teaching and follow Him.

Pray!

Ask God to help you understand what you read in the book of Mark this week.

WEIRD WORDS

Bear grain
Produce seeds

The Twelve
Jesus' twelve disciples

Perceiving
Understanding

76

**Mark
4 v 13-20**

*Remember
Jesus' story from
yesterday?*

*Remind yourself
by checking out
Mark 4 v 1-9.*

*Would you have
hung around
to hear Jesus'
explanation?*

WEIRD WORDS

Parable
Story used by Jesus
to explain a big
truth

Persecution
Hassle for believing
God's word

Deceitfulness
Lies and dishonesty

Top crop

If so, read Mark 4 v 13-20

*Discover's drawing diva, Kirsty,
needs a rest. So it's up to you to
draw the pics and fill in the missing
words today.*

1: Some seed landed on the path
and was munched by the birds.

**The seed is God's w_____
(v14). S_____ takes the
word from people's minds, so
they don't listen to it (v15).**

2: Some seed fell on rocky ground
with only shallow soil. It quickly
grew, but soon withered because
it had no roots.

**That's like people who hear
the message of Jesus and
r_____ it with joy
(v16). But they don't let it
affect their whole lives.
So when t_____ or
p_____ come
along, they quickly
turn away from God (v17).**

3: Some seed fell between thorns
which choked the plants.

**That's like people who let
wo_____, we_____
or the de_____ to
have things become more
important than God (v19).**

4: Some seed fell on good soil and
produced a huge crop!

**That's people who h_____
the message of Jesus,
a_____ it (v20) and let
God change their lives. They
become fruitful for God!**

Pray!

Which seed are you like?
If it's 1, 2 or 3, ask God to help
you listen to His word and let it
change your life.
If you're like seed 4, then thank
God for giving you His awesome
truth to transform your life!

Let it shine

There's a sudden power cut and your whole house is plunged into total darkness.

You stumble around until you find a lamp or flashlight.

What would you do with it?

a) Put it under a bowl ☐

b) Hide it under your bed ☐

c) Put it where it can light up the whole room ☐

Read Mark 4 v 21-23

It would be stupid to hide a light so it can't be seen. You'd put it where it can shine the most.

So what light is Jesus talking about? Go back 1 letter to find out.

_ _ _ _ ,
H P E T

_ _ _ _ : _ _ _
X P S E   U I F

_ _ _ _ _ _
N F T T B H F

_ _   _ _ _ _ _
P G   K F T V T

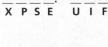

Wow!

Jesus was a shining light to the world. He showed up the world's sin and made it possible for us to be forgiven. His message shouldn't be hidden! It should be allowed to shine EVERYWHERE.

How should the message of Jesus shine?

a) In what we say ☐

b) In how we behave ☐

c) In how we treat other people ☐

We can allow Jesus' message to shine in all of those things! We can tell people about Jesus. We can show kindness and love to people, just as Jesus did. How about giving it a try?

Read verses 24-25

_ _ _ _ _ _ _ _
D P O T J E F S

_ _ _ _ _ _ _ _
D B S F G V M M Z

_ _ _ _   _ _ _
X I B U   Z P V

_ _ _ _ (v24)
I F B S

If we've heard the truth about Jesus, we have **no excuse** for rejecting Him. The more we know of God's word, the more we should obey it and live by it.

WEIRD WORDS

Disclosed
Made known, revealed

Concealed
Hidden

Pray!

Ask God to let Jesus shine through your life. Ask Him to help you obey His word, so you serve Him more.

Gone to seed

**Mark
4 v 26-29**

*Jesus has lots
of stories about
farmers.*

*Here's another
one.*

*It's a short one,
but it teaches us
some great truths.*

Jesus tells us what this parable is
about before He begins.

Read Mark 4 v 26

*To find out, start at the first **T** and
then follow the maze.*

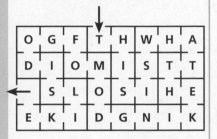

O	G	F	T	H	W	H	A
D	I	O	M	I	S	T	T
	S	L	O	S	I	H	E
E	K	I	D	G	N	I	K

— — — —   — —

— — — —   — — —

— — — — — — —

— —   — — —

— —   — — — —

THE KINGDOM OF GOD

The kingdom of God means all of
God's people — Christians. He is
their King and they are His kingdom,
where He rules! Jesus has made it
possible for anyone to become part
of God's kingdom. And one day
God's people will get to live with
Him. That's when God's kingdom
will be complete.

Read verses 26-29 *and fill in the
gaps.*

A m_____ scatters
s_____ on the ground.
The seed s_____ and
g_____ even though the
man isn't there. When the
crop is r_____ the man
cuts it with his s_____
because the h_____
has come.

1. It's all about Jesus

Jesus is like the man who planted
the seed. When He died and rose
again, He made it possible for us to
become part of God's kingdom. And
even though He's not here on earth
now, God's kingdom continues
to grow as more people become
Christians.

2. Be prepared!

Life may often seem boring and
samey. But be prepared, because
one day Jesus will return. People
who have rejected Him will be
punished. But Jesus will gather all
Christians (like a harvest) to be with
Him forever!

Pray!

Thank God that His kingdom
continues to grow and grow.
Thank Him that one day Jesus will
gather all His people to be with
Him forever.

WEIRD WORDS

Ear/head
Cluster of seeds at
the top of a stalk

Grain/kernel
Centre of a seed,
used for food

Sickle
Sharp tool used to
cut plants (see pic
above)

Cutting the mustard

**Mark
4 v 30-34**

tiny seed

Jesus is still telling parables about seeds.

And He's still telling us about the kingdom of God.

(Remember, God's kingdom means all of God's people — Christians!)

Read Mark 4 v 30-34

Use the backwards word pool to complete Jesus' parable.

dratsum	modgnik
sworg	sdrib
sehcnarb	tseggib
edahs	tsellams

The k_____
of God is like a tiny
m_____ seed. It is
the s_____ of seeds.
Yet it g_____ and
becomes the b_____ of
plants. It's b_____ are
so big that b_____
perch in its s_____.

The kingdom of God started off very small, but will grow and branch out in an amazing way. Jesus knew that nothing could stop God's kingdom from growing.

Find the book of Acts, which shows God's kingdom growing.

Small like a mustard seed

Read Acts 1 v 15

A small group of believers meeting together. Their leader, Jesus, had gone back to heaven.
How many believers were there?

_____

Beginning to grow

Read Acts 2 v 38-41

Jesus gave the Holy Spirit to that small group, enabling them to spread the news about Jesus. About _____ people received God's Word. It completely changed their lives!

Branching out

Read Acts 8 v 4

These believers were persecuted and forced to leave their homes. So they travelled to other countries, telling lots of new people about Jesus!

Today, God's kingdom (the Christian church) is still growing! All over the world, men, women and children have Jesus as the King of their lives. Their hearts and lives are changed by Him.

Pray!

Thank God that His kingdom is still growing. Pray that people you know will turn to God and become part of His kingdom.

**Mark
4 v 35-41**

*Jesus has been
telling lots of
parables to the
people of Galilee.*

*But now it's
time to leave,
and that means
crossing the Sea
of Galilee...*

Shock waves

Read Mark 4 v 35-38

A terrifying storm erupted and
the boat was thrown about. Huge
waves broke over the side of the
boat and the disciples thought they
would drown.

Where was Jesus? (v38)

[blank box]

The disciples woke Jesus up and
accused Him of not caring about
them! What did they say? (v38)

T_____,
don't you c_____
if we d_____?

Read verses 39-41

Jesus stood up and spoke to the
storm. *What happened? (v39)*

[blank box]

What did Jesus say? (v40)

**Why are you
_____? Do you
still have no f_____?**

The disciples didn't realise that Jesus
was God's Son. So they didn't trust
Him to save them. *What did they
say? (v41)*

**W_____ is this? Even
the w_____ and the
w_____ obey Him!**

Jesus has power over everything,
because He is God's Son. Even after
seeing His miracles and hearing His
parables, the disciples still hadn't
worked this out.

Through all these stories about
Jesus, Mark is showing us who Jesus
really is.

Read Mark 1 v 1

The g_____ n_____
about J_____ the
M_____ the
S_____ of G_____

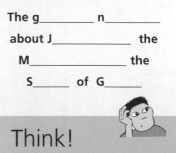

Think!

Do you believe that Jesus is God's
Son? Do you trust Him enough to
let Him have control of your life?

Demon destroyer

**Mark
5 v 1-13**

Jesus has just stopped a violent storm.

Now He comes face to face with a violent man…

WEIRD WORDS

Gerasenes
Area across the lake from Galilee

Irons
Like iron handcuffs that chained your feet together

Subdue
Control

Read Mark 5 v 1-5
and cross out the wrong words.

Jesus and his disciples crossed the lake/river/road. When Jesus got out of the box/BMW/boat, a man with an impolite/impure spirit/spit came to Him from the tombs/combs/trombones. Even though he had often been chewed/chained/beaten up, no one could control him. He wandered through the holes/hippos/hills screaming and cutting himself with stones/paper/scissors.

Impure/evil spirits
Sometimes in the Bible we read about impure/evil spirits. They are God's enemies and often made people ill. But were they more powerful than Jesus?

Read verses 6-10
What did the impure spirits call Jesus? (v7)

S_____ of the M_____
H_____ G_____

Unlike the disciples yesterday, these impure spirits knew that Jesus was God's Son and that He was in charge.

Read verses 11-13
Jesus is far more powerful than impure spirits! So He sent them into a herd of pigs and they were drowned.

Pray!

Jesus is much more powerful than impure/evil spirits, demons and even the devil! Thank God that we don't need to be afraid when Jesus is on our side.

Still scared or worried about impure/evil spirits or the occult? Then write in for our free Occult Fact Sheet. Email: discover@thegoodbook.co.uk

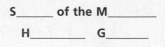

Swine language

Mark
5 v 14-20

Yesterday Jesus met a violent man who was possessed by impure spirits.

Jesus sent the demons into a herd of pigs and they were drowned.

Complete the descriptions to show how Jesus changed the man's life around.

BEFORE
He had __mp__r__ sp__r__ts controlling him. He was v__ __l__nt, no ch__ __ns could hold him, and he went around scr__ __m__ng and c__tt__ng h__ms__lf with st__n__s (Mark 1 v 1-5).

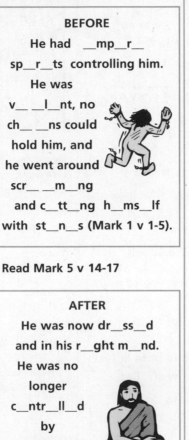

Read Mark 5 v 14-17

AFTER
He was now dr__ss__d and in his r__ght m__nd. He was no longer c__ntr__ll__d by __mp__r__ sp__r__ts.

Wow!

Jesus changes people's lives around! And not just by healing them of illness or impure/evil spirits. If someone turns to Him, Jesus can forgive them so they are no longer controlled by the sin in their life.

Read verses 18-20

What did Jesus tell the man to do? (v19)

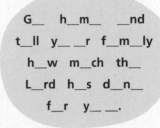
G__ h__m__ __nd t__ll y__ __r f__m__ly h__w m__ch th__ L__rd h__s d__n__ f__r y__ __.

Action!

Has Jesus turned your life around? What has Jesus done in your life? What difference has He made?

_____
_____
_____
_____
_____

Jesus wants you to tell people about what He's done for you!

Pray!

Thank God for all the things you've written down. And ask Him to help you tell people about those great things.

WEIRD WORDS

Legion
Large number

Had mercy on you
Shown you far more kindness than you deserve

Decapolis
10 cities east of Galilee

A woman's touch

**Mark
5 v 21-34**

Another day.

*Another boat
trip across Lake
Galilee.*

Another miracle.

*Another great
lesson from Jesus.*

WEIRD WORDS

Synagogue
Where people met
to learn from the Old
Testament

Earnestly
Seriously

Read Mark 5 v 21-24

and unjumble the anagrams.

J_____ was an
   a i r J u s

important man. He was one
of the s_____
rulers.   o g u n g e y a s

He asked J_____ to
   s u s e J

to heal his d_____
daughter.   g i n d y

*Do you think Jesus will heal his
daughter?*   **YES/NO** _____

Well, we won't find out until
tomorrow! Because, before Jesus
reached Jairus' daughter, someone
else crossed His path…

Read verses 25-34

The woman had been ill for
t_____ years. But
   w e l v e t

no d_____ had
   c o d r o t

been able to heal her; she
only got w_____.
   o r s e w

She touched Jesus'
c_____ and her
   k o a l c

bleeding immediately
s_____!
   p e s t p o d

She believed Jesus could heal her,
even if she just reached out and
touched Him.

What did Jesus say to her? (v34)

Your f_____ has
   h i f a t

h_____ you.
   h a d l e e

Faith is believing that Jesus can help
us. That He's the only one who can
turn our lives around. Because He is
the Son of God.

Pray!

*Father God, thank you that Jesus
can always help me. Thank you
for sending Him into the world,
and that He died to take the
punishment for our sins. Please
help me to have faith in Him.
Amen.*

84

Can Jairus cope?

Mark 5 v 35-43

Yesterday Jesus healed a woman who'd been ill for 12 years!

Before that, He'd met a man called Jairus.

For a reminder of who Jairus was, read Mark 5 v 22-24 and fill in his fact file.

Jairus was one of the s_____ rulers. He fell at Jesus' f_____ and pleaded with Jesus to h_____ his d_____, who was d_____.

But some bad news arrived.

Read verses 35-36

What was the terrible news?

> Your d_____ is d_____

What was Jesus' surprise reply?

> Don't be a_____ just b_____

Jesus told Jairus to trust Him and everything would be alright.

Read verses 37-40

There was chaos at Jairus' h_____. People were c_____ing and w_____ing because the girl was d_____. But Jesus said "The ch_____ is not dead. She is only sl_____". Everyone l_____ed at Him.

None of them **believed** that Jesus could heal the girl. Only Jairus had **faith** in Jesus.

Read verses 41-43

Jesus took the girl by the h_____ and said "T_____ k_____!" which means "get up!" She immediately got up and w_____ed around. Everyone was a_____ed

Wow!

Jesus has power over death! He brought the girl back to life. And if we trust Him, we don't have to fear death either. People who trust in Jesus will live with Him for ever!

Pray!

Praise and thank Jesus that He has power over death.

Jonah: The runaway

**Jonah
1 v 1-3**

*Ever disobeyed
your parents?*

*Let me guess,
your answer
begins with a Y!*

*It's really
tempting to rebel
and disobey
authority.*

*Today we meet
Jonah, who
rebelled against
God.*

*Not such a wise
idea!*

JONAH FACTS

• Jonah lived almost 800 years
before Jesus

• He was an Israelite — one of
God's special people

• He was a prophet — that's a
messenger for God

• His job was to tell people what
God wanted to say to them

• But Jonah wasn't very good at his
job…

Read Jonah 1 v 1-2

*Fill in the vowels (aeiou) to complete
God's orders to Jonah.*

G_ t_
N_n_v_h _nd
pr_ _ch _g_ _nst
it b_c_ _s_ of its
w_ck_dn_ss

NINEVEH FACTS

• Nineveh was a city full of people
who rejected God

• It was in Assyria, a hated enemy of
the Israelites

• God sent Jonah to tell them to
start living His way

• God planned for other people (not
just the Israelites) to know Him
and serve Him too

• But Jonah and the Israelites
wanted God all for themselves

Read Jonah 1 v 3

So what did Jonah do?

R_n _w_y fr_m
th_ L_rd _nd
w_nt t_ T_rsh_sh

Tarshish was probably in Spain, the
opposite direction to Nineveh!

Think!

Ever run away from God? Doing the
opposite of what He wants you to
do? How?

_____

_____

_____

_____

Pray!

Ask God to help you learn how to
obey Him more as you read the
book of Jonah.

Stormy weather

**Jonah
1 v 4-10**

God told Jonah to go and preach in Nineveh.

Jonah ran off in the opposite direction.

But it's impossible to run away from God!

Read Jonah 1 v 4-6

Unjumble the anagrams to reveal what happened.

The L_____ sent a
d r o L

great w_____ and a
d i w n

violent s_____ that
m o r s t

looked like breaking up the

entire s_____!
h i p s

Jonah tried to run away from God, but God was in total control. The wind and the waves obeyed Him. The sailors prayed to their own fake gods, but only God is real and in total control.

Want more proof?

Read verse 7

The s_____ cast
s o s r a i l

l_____ to see who was
s t o l

r_____.
b o r i s s p l e e n

The lot fell on J_____.
n a J o h

God was in charge. He made sure the sailors knew that Jonah had caused the storm by running away from Him.

Read verses 8-10

The sailors wanted to know who Jonah was and why the storm was happening. *What was Jonah's answer?*

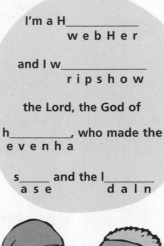

I'm a H_____
w e b H e r

and I w_____
r i p s h o w

the Lord, the God of

h_____, who made the
e v e n h a

s_____ and the l_____
a s e   d a l n

Jonah claimed to serve God but was running away from Him!

Wow!

We can't run away from God because He's in total control of everything. We can't outsmart the God who made the whole universe!

Pray!

Thank God that He's in control of our lives. Say sorry for the times you run away from Him and live your own way.

Man overboard

**Jonah
1 v 11-17**

*Jonah's on the
run from God.*

*But God's in total
control and won't
let Jonah off the
hook!*

Read Jonah 1 v 11-12

*What did Jonah say the sailors
should do?*

Leave him alone ☐

Throw him into the sea ☐

Catch fish for lunch ☐

Maybe Jonah had finally realised he
couldn't run away from God.

Read verse 13

The men didn't want to send Jonah
to his death so they rowed even
harder. But the storm got even
wilder!

Read verses 14-16

What did the sailors do?

Prayed to God and threw
fish overboard ☐

Played golf and threw
Jonah overboard ☐

Prayed to God and threw
Jonah overboard ☐

Then what happened?

The ship sank ☐

The sea grew calm ☐

Jonah swam to Tarshish ☐

God was in complete control of the
situation. His plan for Jonah to go to
Nineveh had not stopped. But Jonah
was learning this the hard way!

Read verse 17

*What did God send to stop Jonah
from drowning?*

A big whale ☐

A large stork ☐

A huge fish ☐

WEIRD WORDS

Accountable
Responsible and
deserving to be
punished

Vows
Promises

Pray!

Praise God that He is always in
charge of events and that His
perfect plans cannot be stopped!

Inside the fish

**Jonah
2 v 1-10**

*God wanted
Jonah to take
His message to
Nineveh.*

*But Jonah tried to
run away.*

WEIRD WORDS

Currents
Dangerous parts of
the sea

Breakers
Big waves

Banished
Sent away

Engulfing
Flowing over and
surrounding

Idols
False gods

Salvation
Rescue

Yet God wouldn't let him. Jonah
was trapped in a violent storm,
thrown overboard and now he's
in a fish's stomach! No wonder his
attitude changed towards God…

Read Jonah 2 v 1-9
Jonah's prayer teaches us some
great truths about God.

1. God hears our cries (v2)
Jonah was drowning in the sea and
he cried out to God for help. God
heard him and rescued him.

**God hears our cries too. When
we call Him, He hears and
answers us. Not always in the
way we expect, but He does
always answer.**

2. God's in control (v3)
Jonah realised that God had caused
the storm, and was in charge even
when he was drowning.

**God rules the whole universe!
He's in charge of everything!**

3. God forgives (v4)
God sent a violent storm because
Jonah tried to run away from Him.
But He didn't let Jonah die. From
inside the fish's belly, Jonah knew
he would live to worship God again!

**When we run away from God,
we can always turn back to Him.
We can say sorry and ask Him to
forgive us!**

4. God rescues (v5-6)
God sent a huge fish to swallow
Jonah and rescue him!

**And God can rescue us too. He
sent His Son, Jesus, to die in our
place. So everyone who trusts
Him will be rescued from sin and
the punishment of hell!**

5. Only one God (v8)
Jonah has shown us how awesome
God is.

**So putting anything else first
in your life would be crazy! We
should worship God and nothing
else!**

Read verse 10
Yuck! The fish vomited Jonah! God
had brought Jonah to safety!

Pray!

Spend time thanking God for
these 5 great truths we've learned
about Him today.

Prophet and loss

**Jonah
3 v 1-4**

*God has given
Jonah a second
chance.*

*He rescued Jonah
from the sea
and commanded
a large fish to
throw him up
onto dry land!*

WEIRD WORDS

Proclaim
Tell everyone

Overthrown
Destroyed

Read Jonah 3 v 1-3

God gave Jonah the same orders
He'd given him earlier. *Reveal them
by going back one letter.*

H P   U P

O J O F W F I

B O E   U F M M

U I F N   U I F

N F T T B H F   J

H J W F   Z P V

This time Jonah obeyed God and
went to Nineveh!

Wow!

We've all let God down loads. But
we can still turn around and start
living for Him again.

Read verse 4

*What was God's terrifying message
to the people of Nineveh?*

J O   5 1   E B Z T

O J O F W F I

X J M M   C F

E F T U S P Z F E

Imagine hearing that terrifying
news! But these people had
disobeyed God and refused to live
for Him. So God told them they
would get the punishment they
deserved.

Wow!

God is fair. Everyone has the chance
to live His way. But God doesn't
take sin lightly. And He promises to
punish anyone who rejects Him.

But that's not the end of it!
He also gives everyone a way of
avoiding His punishment. Tomorrow
we'll see if the people of Nineveh
took that way out…

Pray!

Thank God for messengers like
Jonah. Who has taught you from
God's word, the Bible?

_____

_____

_____

Spend time thanking God for
them and praying for them.

90

Jonah 3 v 5-10

Jonah has delivered God's message: Nineveh will be destroyed in 40 days.

Getting the sack

Check out the surprise reaction.

Read Jonah 3 v 5-9

All today's answers can be found in the wordsearch.

```
C F D E T N E L E R
S O N I N E V E H B
A Q M B P C I L A E
C Z F P G O L W R L
K I N G A T T D K I
C E Q E T S R M N E
L P S V U A S B H V
O C J D O F J I S E
T U R N E D N G O D
H L D E S T R O Y N
```

What did the people do?

- B_____ God (v5)
- Decided to f_____ (v5)
- Started wearing s_____ (v5)
- Even the k_____ joined in (v6)
- They called to G_____ (v8)
- Gave up their e_____ ways (v8)

They stopped sinning against God, started living for Him and asked Him to forgive them.

Wow!

Becoming a Christian involves turning away from sin, asking God to forgive you and starting to live for Him.

Read verse 10

When God saw they'd t_____ from their evil ways He r_____ and did not d_____ the city of N_____

Wow!

God is amazingly loving and forgiving. When people turn away from sin and turn to Him, He forgives them and gives them a new start!

Pray!

Thank God that we can be forgiven even though we've sinned against Him. Praise Him for loving us so much.

Want to live more for God? For help in how to grow as a Christian email: discover@thegoodbook.co.uk

Incredible sulk

**Jonah
4 v 1-4**

Think of someone you know who's not, er, a very nice person.

Someone who's a real pain to you.

WEIRD WORDS

Forestall
Put off happening

Gracious
Giving people far more than they deserve

Compassionate
Loving and caring

Abounding in
Full of

Calamity
Disaster and misery

Now imagine that person suddenly becoming a Christian and turning away from all the bad stuff they did.

How would you feel about that?

I hope you wouldn't feel like Jonah did about Nineveh.

Read Jonah 4 v 1-4

and tick the sentences that describe Jonah's reaction.

Pleased for Nineveh ☐

Angry with God ☐

Upset that Nineveh had been forgiven ☐

Not really bothered ☐

Wanted to die ☐

Dancing with joy ☐

Jonah didn't want God to forgive the people of Nineveh. He wanted to see the city destroyed. He wanted God only to show His love to the Israelites, not to other people too.

Think!

Do you want other people to get to know God? Or would you rather keep God to yourself?

Unjumble the anagrams to show how Jonah described God (v2).

G_____
r a G i c u s o

C_____
i a t e m a n s s C o o p

Slow to a_____
r a n g e

Abounding in l_____
e v o l

Wow!

God is all of those things. And so He loves it when people turn away from sin and start living for Him. He longs to forgive them!

Pray!

Thank God that He's so forgiving. And pray for the person you thought of earlier. Pray that they'll say sorry to God and He'll forgive them.

Worm food

92

**Jonah
4 v 5-11**

*The people of
Nineveh have
turned to God!*

*So God is going
to let them
live, instead of
destroying the
city!*

*But miserable
Jonah wished that
God would punish
them.*

So God taught Jonah an important
lesson.

Read Jonah 4 v 5-8

and fill in the vowels (aeiou).

- J__n__h w__nt and s__t
  d__wn east of the c__ty,
  w__ __t__ng to see what
  would h__pp__n.

- The L__rd G__d made a
  l__ __fy plant gr__w up
  over Jonah to give him
  sh__d__ from the s__n.

- At d__wn the n__xt d__y,
  God sent a w__rm which
  ch__w__d the plant until
  it w__th__r__d.

- God sent a hot east w__nd
  and the s__n bl__z__d on
  Jonah's h__ __d until he
  w__nt__d to d__ __.

What could Jonah possibly learn
from that harsh lesson?

Read verses 9-11

What did God say to Jonah?

- You've been c__nc__rn__d
  about this pl__nt even
  though you didn't m__k__
  it gr__w. It spr__ng up
  __v__rn__ght and then
  d__ __d __v__rn__ght.

- But N__n__v__h has more
  than a h__ndr__d __nd
  tw__nty th__ __s__nd
  p__ __ple. Should I not be
  concerned about Nineveh?!

Jonah cared about a plant, yet he
didn't care for a city full of people!
But God cared deeply for the 1000s
of people (and animals) in Nineveh.
God didn't want them to die, so He
was overjoyed when they turned to
Him.

Pray!

Do you care for the people
around you? Do you care that
many of them don't know God?
Write down people you want to
turn to God (include people you
don't enjoy being around!)

_____

_____

_____

Spend time praying that God will
turn their lives around.

DISCOVER
COLLECTION

ISSUE 2

DISCOVER ISSUE 2

Grab hold of God's great promises in Genesis. Meet Jesus, the sensational Saviour, in Mark. Listen in as Elisha tells God's people what they need to hear. And let Philippians challenge you to really live for Jesus every day.

COLLECT 12 THE SET

COLLECT ALL 12 ISSUES TO COMPLETE THE DISCOVER COLLECTION

Don't forget to order the next issue of Discover. Or even better, grab a one-year subscription to make sure Discover lands in your hands as soon as it's out. Packed full of puzzles, prayers and pondering points.

thegoodbook.co.uk thegoodbook.com

thegoodbook
COMPANY